INSPIRATIONS BOOKS

MANAGING EDITOR Sue Gardner

EDITOR-IN-CHIEF Coral Moss

EDITOR Margie Bauer

PATTERN DESIGNER Sarah Kent

EDITORIAL ASSISTANTS
Marian Carpenter, Lizzie Kulinski,
Heather Moody, Susan O'Connor,
Joy Peters, Wendy Sysouphat

STYLIST Gai Kerkez

PROPS Fiona Fagan

GRAPHIC DESIGN Lynton Grandison

ILLUSTRATIONS
Kathy Barac, Wendy Sysouphat

PHOTOGRAPHY Andrew Dunbar

REPROGRAPHICS van Gastel Graphics

PUBLISHER Margie Bauer

THE WORLD'S MOST
BEAUTFUL EMBROIDERED BLANKETS
ISBN 0-9579069-4-3

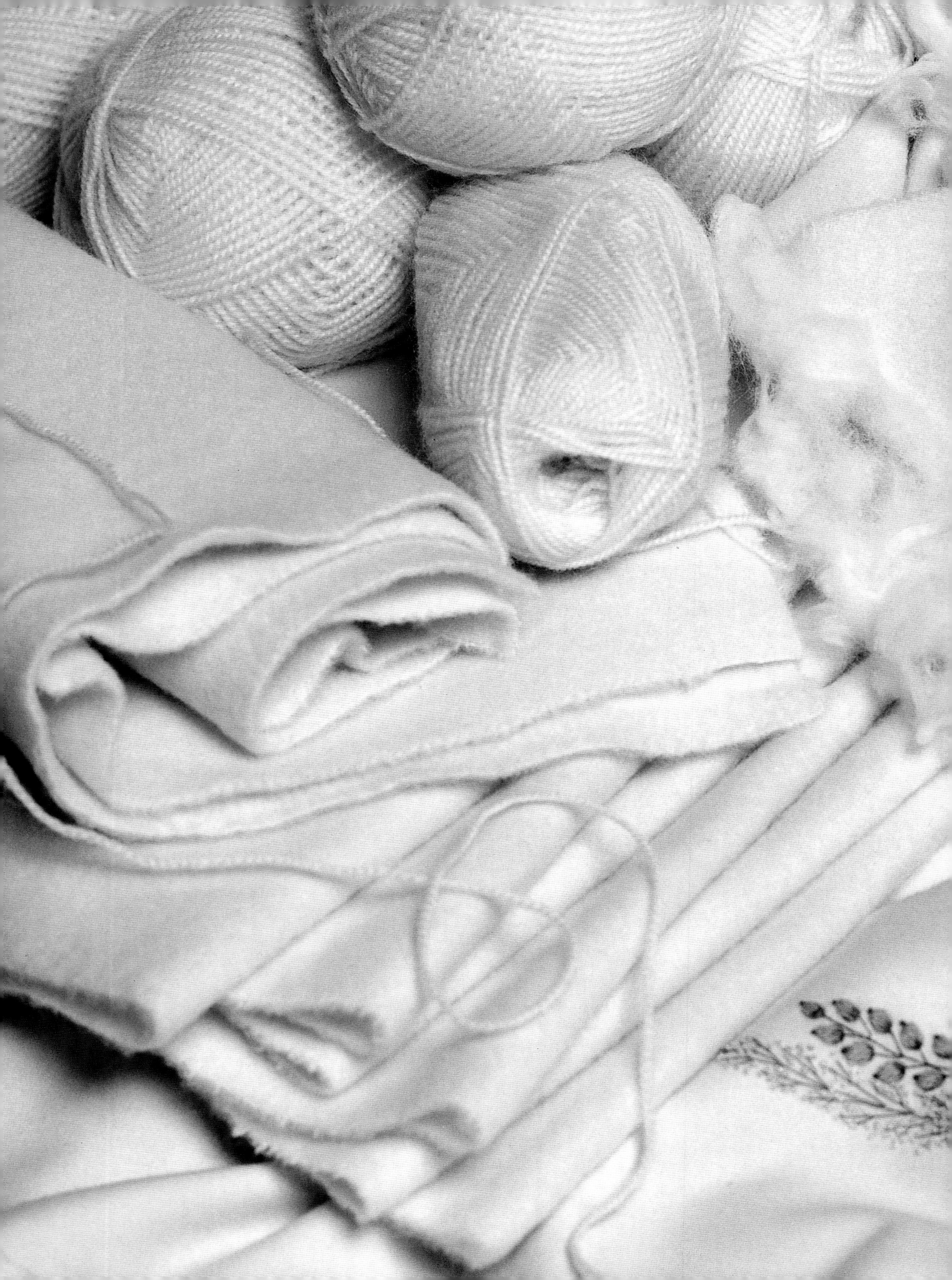

The
world's most beautiful
embroidered
Blankets

CONTENTS

It's not enough to weave beautiful rugs. You have to think beautiful thoughts while weaving them.

Charles Loloma, Hopi

Clusters of lavish pink roses bloom at each corner of this elegant blanket. A rich scalloped border, reminiscent of lace, is embroidered around the edge and lines of stem stitch intersect to form a subtle lattice. Pink buds are scattered across the surface. The blanket is backed and the curved edges are bound with silk and cotton twill.

REQUIREMENTS

Fabric

112cm x 140cm wide (44" x 55") piece of ivory wool and cashmere velour

1.9m x 112cm wide (2yd 3" x 44") cream cotton and silk twill

Supplies

30cm (12") quilting hoop

Tracing paper

Water-soluble fabric marker

Medium black permanent pen

Threads & Needle

See page 16.

THIS DESIGN USES

Detached chain stitch
Fly stitch, French knot
Long and short stitch
Outline stitch, Satin stitch
Stem stitch

• • •

PREPARATION FOR EMBROIDERY

See page 127 for transferring the design and the pattern sheet for the scallop template, embroidery designs and lattice diagram.

"Of all the woollen fabrics available, the magical blend of cosy wool and luxurious cashmere is my favourite.

This fabric is a dream to use, translucent enough to trace designs through and with a beautiful smooth velour surface that doesn't overwhelm the stitches."

Susan

The finished blanket measures 132cm x 104cm wide (52" x 41")

Embroidery

See page 17 for the step-by-step instructions for stitching a thread painted rose and the pattern sheet for the stitch direction diagram.

The border and lattice are worked with the fabric out of the hoop. Place the fabric in the hoop when working the rose sprays and buds.

Order of work

Lace border

Stitch the large and small scalloped lines with stem stitch. Fill the small scallops with partial daisies in detached chain. For each, work the central petal first and then the side petals. Fill the spaces between *(diag 1)*.

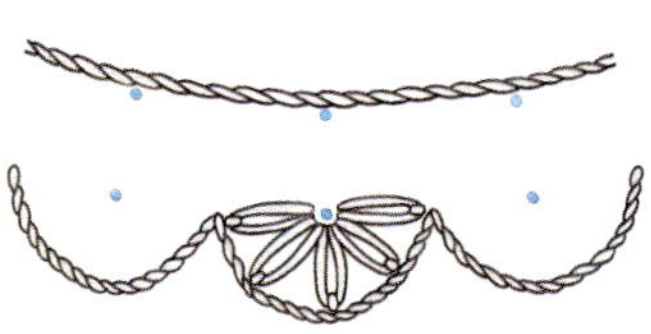

Diag 1

At the junction of each set of small scallops, work the daisy with three petals only *(diag 2)*.

Diag 2

Referring to the lace border photograph, work the remaining partial daisies with three petals. Add the French knots.

Work fly stitch evenly around the outside of the small scallops.

Lattice

Embroider the lattice lines with stem stitch. Embellish each intersection with partial daisies using detached chains and French knots *(diag 3)*.

Diag 3

Work the partial daisies at the peaks of the large scallops with a slightly different number of petals *(diag 4)*.

Diag 4

Rose spray

Embroider the rose following the step-by-step instructions. Work the leaves in long and short stitch and satin stitch, changing colour as indicated in the photograph.

Embroider the bud sepal outlines with stem stitch. Fill with satin or long and short stitch. Work the bud petals in satin or long and short stitch.

Scattered buds

Stitch the scattered buds in the same manner, working the stems with a row of stem stitch, then outline stitch. Add the receptacle in satin stitch or long and short stitch.

Construction

See pages 127 and 128.

"THERE IS TIME FOR WORK. AND TIME FOR LOVE. THAT LEAVES NO TIME."

GABRIELLE (COCO) CHANEL

Threads *and* Needle

Paterna Persian yarn

A = 263 cream (15 skeins)
B = 641 dk khaki green
C = 642 med khaki green
D = 643 khaki green
E = 653 olive green
F = 692 med loden green
G = 693 loden green
H = 694 lt loden green
I = 930 vy dk rusty rose
J = 931 dk rusty rose
K = 933 rusty rose (2 skeins)
L = 934 lt rusty rose (2 skeins)
M = 935 vy lt rusty rose (2 skeins)
N = 948 ultra vy lt cranberry (2 skeins)

Needle

No. 18 chenille needle

Embroidery Key

All embroidery is worked with one strand of yarn.

Lace

Border = A (stem stitch, fly stitch, detached chain, French knot, 1 wrap)

Lattice = A (stem stitch, detached chain, French knot, 1 wrap)

Rose spray

Rose = K, L, M and N (long and short stitch), L (satin stitch), K (satin stitch, stem stitch)

Bud 1

Sepals = D, F and H (stem stitch, long and short stitch), C (stem stitch, satin stitch)

Petals = I and J (long and short stitch)

Bud 2

Sepals = B, D and F (stem stitch, long and short stitch)

Petals = I and J (long and short stitch)

Bud 3

Sepals = B, C and D (stem stitch, long and short stitch), H (long and short stitch)

Petals = I (satin stitch)

Bud 4

Sepals = C, D and G (stem stitch, long and short stitch), E (long and short stitch)

Leaf 1 = C, F, G and H (long and short stitch, satin stitch)

Leaves 2 and 4 = C, D and E (long and short stitch, satin stitch)

Leaf 3 = C, F and G (long and short stitch, satin stitch)

Scattered buds

Bud 5

Stem = G (outline stitch, stem stitch)

Receptacle = G and D (satin stitch)

Sepals = D, E, G and H (stem stitch, long and short stitch, satin stitch)

Petals = J (satin stitch)

Bud 6

Stem = D (outline stitch, stem stitch)

Receptacle = D and E (satin stitch)

Sepals = D, E and H (stem stitch, long and short stitch, satin stitch)

Petals = I and J (long and short stitch)

Bud 7

Stem = H (outline stitch, stem stitch)

Receptacle = H (satin stitch)

Sepals = F, G and H (stem stitch, long and short stitch, satin stitch)

Petals = I and J (long and short stitch)

Bud 8

Stem = G (outline stitch, stem stitch)

Receptacle = F and G (satin stitch)

Sepals = D, F and G (stem stitch, long and short stitch, satin stitch)

Petals = J (long and short stitch, satin stitch)

Bud 9

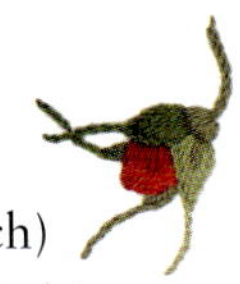

Stem = D (outline stitch, stem stitch)

Receptacle = D (satin stitch)

Sepals = D, F and H (stem stitch, long and short stitch, satin stitch)

Petals = I and J (long and short stitch)

Bud 10

Stem = E (outline stitch, stem stitch)

Receptacle = E (satin stitch)

Sepals = D, E and G (stem stitch, long and short stitch, satin stitch)

Petals = J (satin stitch)

Bud 11

Stem = D (outline stitch, stem stitch)

Receptacle = D and G (satin stitch)

Sepals = D, F, G and H (stem stitch, long and short stitch, satin stitch)

Petals = I and J (long and short stitch)

Bud 12

Stem = G (outline stitch, stem stitch)

Receptacle = G and F (satin stitch)

Sepals = D, F, and G (stem stitch, long and short stitch, satin stitch)

Petals = J (satin stitch)

Thread Painted Rose

1. Outer petals. Using L, fill the narrow petal with satin stitch.

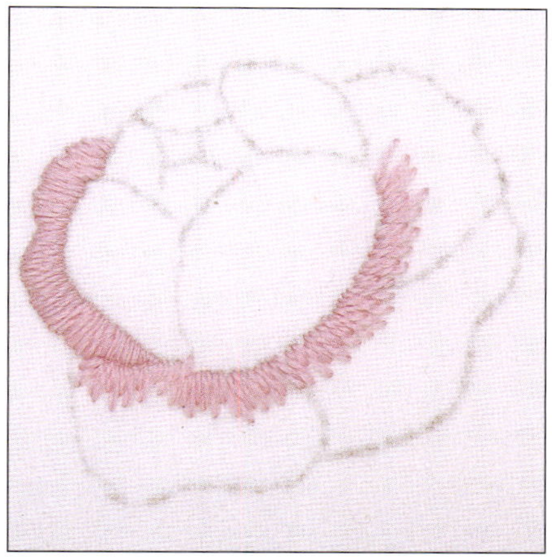

2. Work a row of long and short stitch along the inside edge of each outer petal.

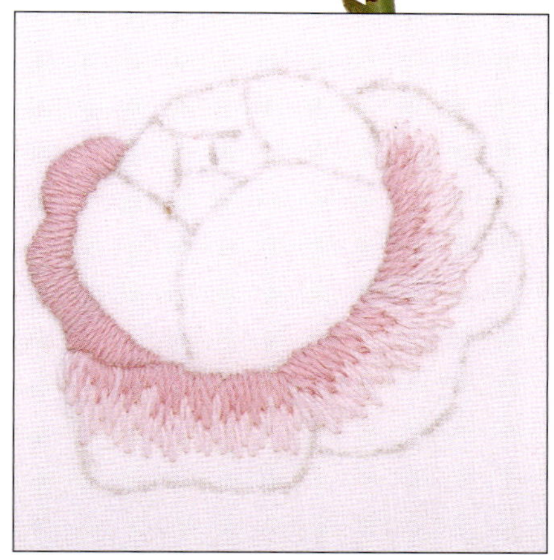

3. Using M, stitch a row of long and short stitch along the middle of the outer petals.

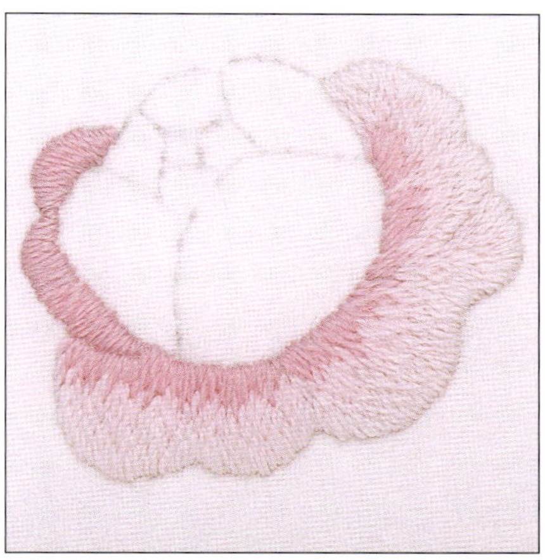

4. Using N, fill the remaining area of each outer petal in long and short stitch.

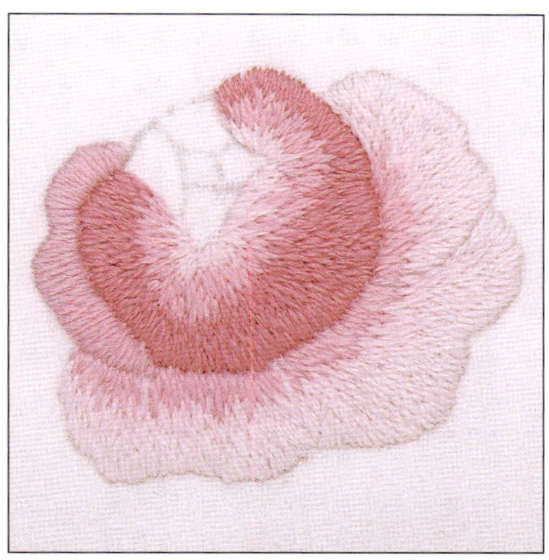

5. Inner petals. Fill the three large inner petals in the same manner using M first, then L and K.

6. Using K, stitch the centre in satin stitch. Work the outer edge of the small inner petals in long and short stitch.

7. Fill the remaining area with L.

8. Using K, outline the edges of the inner petals and the divisions between the outer petals in stem stitch.

9. Work spaced long and short stitches over the inner edges of the outer petals with K.

Superb blooms of delicate pink and white appear ready to be picked from this dazzling dark navy wool and cashmere blanket. Elegant Japanese windflowers are created using a combination of shaded wools highlighted with lustrous silk and rayon threads. Tall flower stems are clothed with leaves in softest shades of green and the open flowers are interspersed with plump pink buds. Shaded ribbon forms a frame for the design and the blanket is finished with a rich purple border.

Requirements

Fabric

105cm x 110cm wide (42" x 43") piece of navy wool and cashmere velour

117cm x 122cm wide (46" x 48") piece of purple cotton print

Supplies

3.5m x 22mm wide (3yd 30" x 7/8") variegated purple wired ribbon

40cm (16") square of white felt

40cm (16") square of white medium weight non-woven fusible interfacing

30cm (12") quilting hoop

White tissue paper

Chalk based fabric marker

Sharp HB pencil

Threads & Needles

See page 27.

This Design Uses

Back stitch, Blanket stitch

Bullion loop, Chain stitch

Detached blanket stitch

Feather stitch, Fly stitch

French knot

Long and short blanket stitch

Long and short stitch

Padded satin stitch

Satin stitch, Stem stitch

Straight stitch

Twisted chain stitch

Preparation for Embroidery

See page 128 for preparing the fabric and the pattern sheet for the embroidery designs and templates for the padded flowers.

Transferring the design

Stems and leaves

Using the pencil, trace the stems and leaves onto the tissue paper three times. Position one tracing along the vertical centre line on the right side of the blanketing, matching placement marks with the lower line of tacking and pin in place.

Tack along the outlines of the leaves, using contrasting machine sewing thread and very small tacking stitches. Using larger tacking stitches, tack along each stem.

Lightly moisten the tissue paper with a damp sponge, wait a few seconds, then carefully remove the paper.

THE FINISHED BLANKET MEASURES 105CM X 110CM WIDE (42" X 43")

Mark the central vein for each leaf with the chalk based fabric marker.

Using the remaining two tracings, place one at each side of the central stem, with its main stem 21cm (8 1/4") away from the first. Transfer the designs in the same manner as before.

Flowers

Trace the flowers, buds and small stems onto the tissue paper. Position the tracing above the top two tacked leaves, aligning the placement marks with the lines of tacking. Pin in place. Tack along the stems and mark the centre of each flower and bud with a small tacked circle. Do not tack around the flower outlines. Remove the tissue paper as before.

Trace the flowers and buds onto the interfacing. Cut out the shapes around the outer edge and, using a protective cloth, fuse them onto the blanket at the marked positions.

"The interfacing prevents the navy fabric from showing through the embroidery stitches." ANNIE

Embroidery

See the pattern sheet for the flower templates. See the step-by-step instructions on pages 28 and 29 for working the fly stitch and feather stitch leaves, the twisted chain stitch stems and the windflowers.

Use the no. 9 milliner's needle when working with the silk threads and the no. 5 milliner's needle for the bullion knots and French knots. Use the no. 20 chenille needle for the twisted chain stem and the no. 24 chenille needle for all other embroidery.

Work all embroidery in the hoop except for the bullion loops and the detached blanket stitch.

Order of work

Leaves

The leaves are embroidered using three different stitches to add variation to the design. When working the satin stitch leaves, begin with a straight stitch at the tip and work angled satin stitches to the base.

satin stitch

fly stitch

For the fly stitch leaves, vary the spacing of the stitches from leaf to leaf.

feather stitch

Only two leaves are worked in feather stitch.

Stems

Working down the stem, embroider the three main stems in twisted chain stitch and the flower stems in chain stitch.

Work the remaining stems, including those without leaves and the two on the fallen buds, in back stitch or stem stitch.

Grass

Work the grass with straight stitches, forming clumps.

Ground cover

Scatter French knots along the base of the flower stems using a random selection of colours.

Flowers

Following the step-by-step instructions, work the full flowers, some with the variations.

Work the side view flowers in a similar manner, with green French knots replacing the satin stitch on the outer centre.

Buds

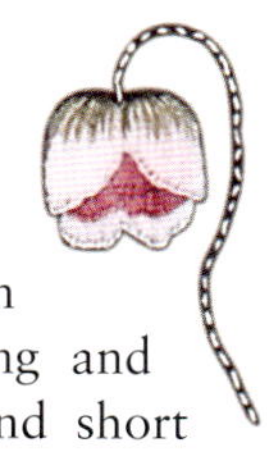

Work the opening buds in a similar manner to the petals of the flowers. For the closed and fallen buds, attach the padding and then cover with long and short stitch and straight stitch highlights.

Construction

See page 128.

Left hand flower

Middle flower

Leaves of middle flower

– Threads and Needles –

Gumnut Yarns 'Daisies' fine wool

A = 076 med dk carnation
B = 191 ultra lt ripe plum
C = 193 lt ripe plum
D = 195 med ripe plum
E = 232 vy lt pansy
F = 641 ultra lt khaki
G = 643 lt khaki (2 skeins)
H = 645 med khaki (2 skeins)
I = 646 dk khaki (2 skeins)
J = 991 ecru (5 skeins)

Gumnut Yarns 'Buds' perlé silk

K = 643 lt khaki (2 skeins)
L = 645 med khaki

Rajmahal stranded rayon

M = 45 baby camel
N = 200 barely pink
O = 243 grape
P = 421 green earth

Edmar 'Glory' rayon

Q = 129 gold

Anchor Marlitt rayon

R = 867 golden yellow

Needles

No. 5 milliner's needle
No. 9 milliner's needle
No. 20 chenille needle
No. 24 chenille needle

– Embroidery Key –

All embroidery is worked with one strand unless otherwise specified.

Leaves

Leaves 1, 2 and 9 = K (straight stitch, fly stitch)
Leaves 3 and 6 = G (satin stitch)
Leaf 4 = I (1 or 2 strands, straight stitch, fly stitch)
Leaf 5 = H (1 or 2 strands, straight stitch, fly stitch or 2 strands, feather stitch)

Leaves 7 and 10 = G or I (straight stitch, fly stitch)
Leaf 8 = I (feather stitch or straight stitch, fly stitch)
Leaf 11 = H (1 or 2 strands, straight stitch, fly stitch)

Stems of leaves

Main stems = L (4 strands, twisted chain stitch)
Leaves 3, 6 and 10 = K (back stitch)
Leaves 4, 5, 8, 9 and 11 = L (stem stitch)
Leaf 7 = L (back stitch)

Stems of flowers = K (chain stitch)
Stems of buds = K (back stitch)
Remaining stems = K (stem stitch)
Grass = G, I, K and P (straight stitch)
Ground cover = A, C, D, F, G, H, I, J, K and L (French knot, 2 - 3 wraps)

Flowers

Back petals = J (blanket stitch)
Front petals = J (long and short blanket stitch, long and short stitch)
Highlights = B, E and N or B, D and N (straight stitch)
Between petals = F (straight stitch)
Edge of some front petals = J (detached blanket stitch)

Centre of full flower

Inner = G and P (padded satin stitch)
Outer = G or H (satin stitch)
Inner outline = P (2 strands, back stitch)
Highlights = P (straight stitch)
Stamens = M, Q and R (French knot, 2 - 3 wraps)
Pink loops = B (bullion loop, 30 wraps)

Centre of half flower

Inner = G and P (padded satin stitch)
Outer = G, K and P (French knot, 1 - 3 wraps)
Stamens = M, Q and R (French knots, 2 - 3 wraps)

Buds

Buds 1 and 2

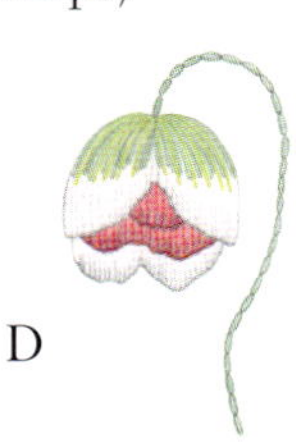

Back petals = B or C (blanket stitch)
Middle petals = A or D (blanket stitch)
Front petals = B (blanket stitch, straight stitch)
Calyx = I (straight stitch)
Calyx highlights = P (straight stitch)

Bud 3

Back petals = A (blanket stitch), I (straight stitch)
Front petals = B and C (blanket stitch, straight stitch)
Calyx = I (straight stitch)
Calyx highlights = P (straight stitch)

Buds 4 and 5

Petals = D (blanket stitch, straight stitch), I (straight stitch)
Petal highlights = O (straight stitch)
Calyx = I (long and short stitch), P (straight stitch)

Bud 6 and lower right fallen bud

Petals = D (satin stitch)
Petal highlights = O (straight stitch)
Calyx = I (straight stitch)
Calyx highlights = P (straight stitch)

Buds 7, 8 and lower left fallen bud

Petals = D (straight stitch)
Petal highlights = O (straight stitch)
Calyx = G and I (straight stitch)
Calyx highlights = P (straight stitch)

Fly Stitch Leaf

Fly stitch is a single looped stitch that forms a Y shape. A number of fly stitches can be worked in a line to form a very effective leaf.

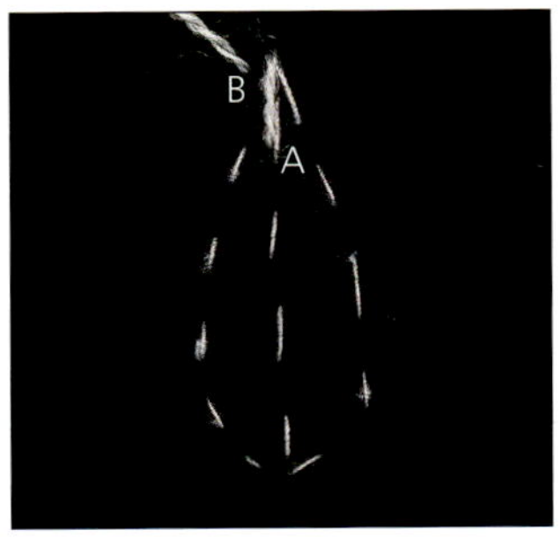

1. Mark the outline and vein. Work a straight stitch from the tip to A. Bring the thread to the front at B, just below the tip.

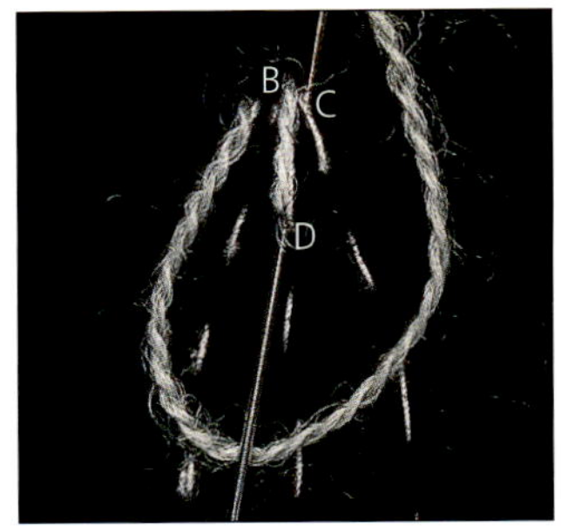

2. Take to the back at C. With the thread under the needle, bring to the front at D on the centre vein.

3. Tighten the loop. Take to the back at E, anchoring the first fly stitch. Emerge at F.

4. Continue filling the shape, changing the angle of the stitches slightly to suit the outline.

5. When the shape is filled, work the last anchoring stitch longer to form a stem if required.

Feather Stitch Leaf

Feather stitch creates a leaf with a lacy central vein. The slanted needle position alternates from side to side as you stitch.

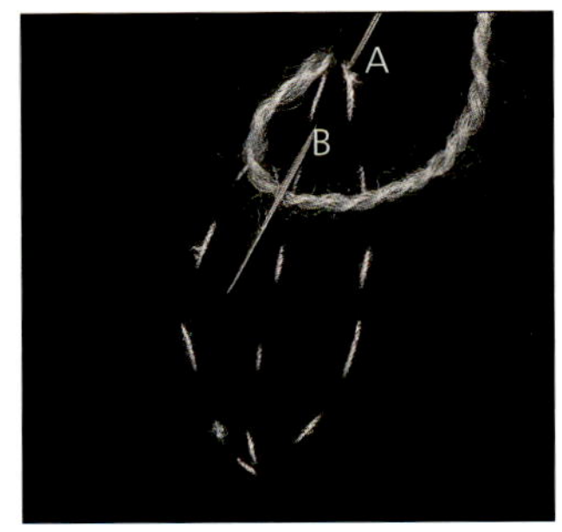

1. Bring the needle to the front at the leaf tip. With the thread under the needle, take it from A to B at the right of the vein.

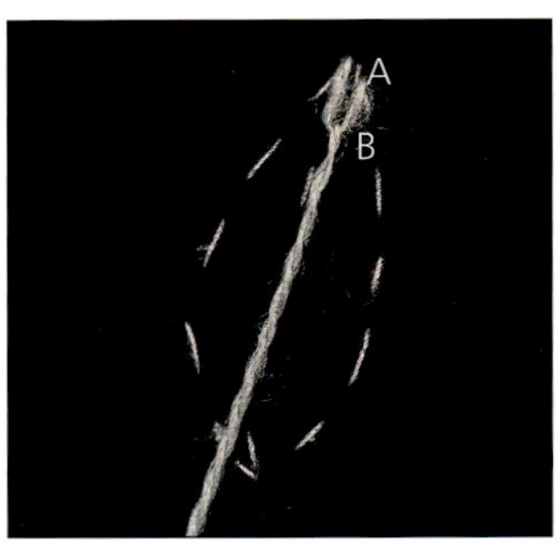

2. Pull the thread through in a downward movement.

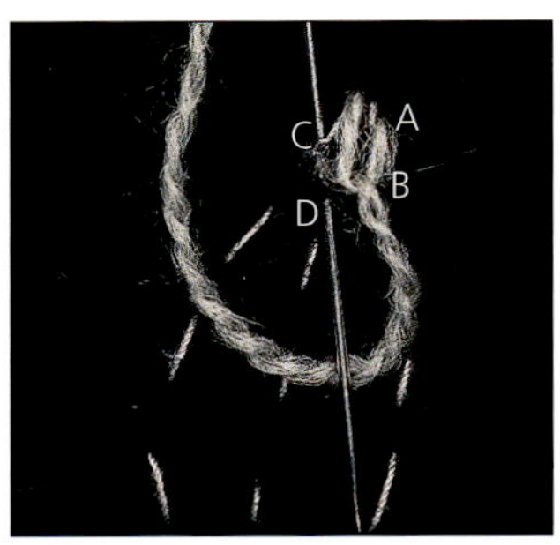

3. Work a stitch slanting down from C. Emerge slightly to the left of the vein, at D. Ensure that the thread is under the needle.

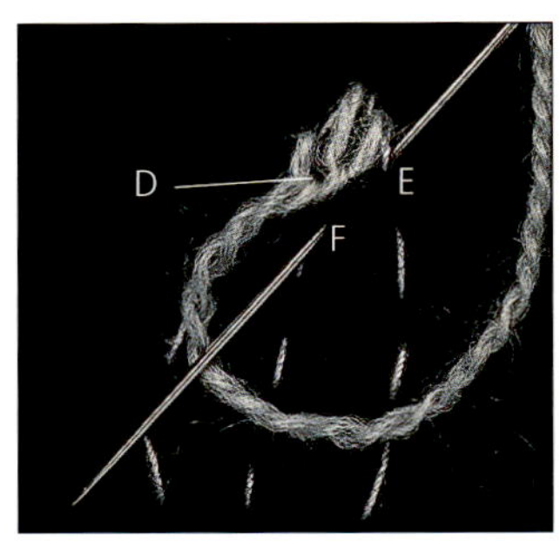

4. Pull the thread through and continue in the same manner, working another slanting stitch from E to F.

5. Continue filling the leaf shape. Work the last anchoring stitch longer to form a stem if required.

Twisted Chain Stitch Stem

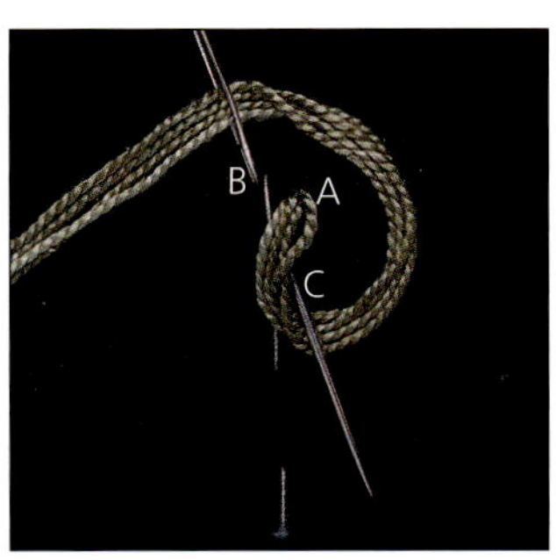

1. Bring thread to front at A. Take needle to back at B. Emerge at C, forming a twisted loop.

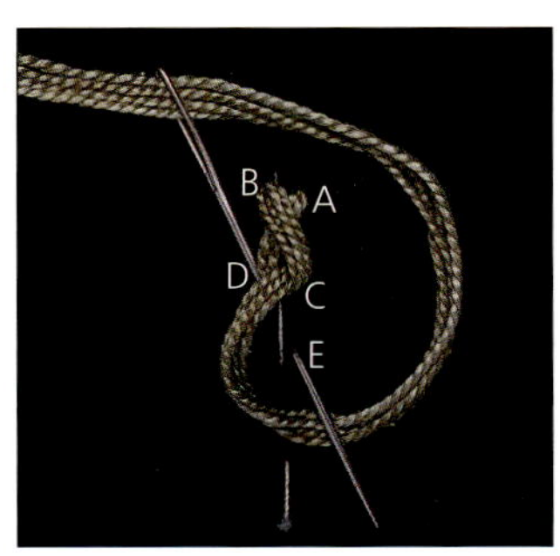

2. Pull the thread through. Take the needle from D to E with the thread under the needle tip.

3. Continue stitching the required distance. To end off, take the needle to the back just below the last loop.

Japanese Windflower

The use of a variety of stitches and raised techniques results in a dramatic three dimensional effect for the windflowers.

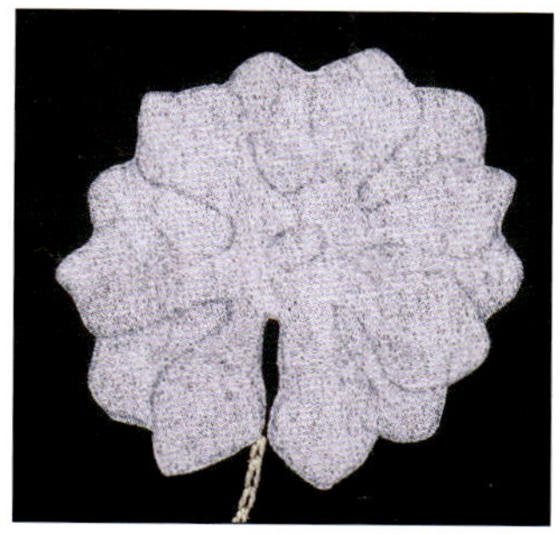

1. Base petals. Fuse the interfacing shape in place.

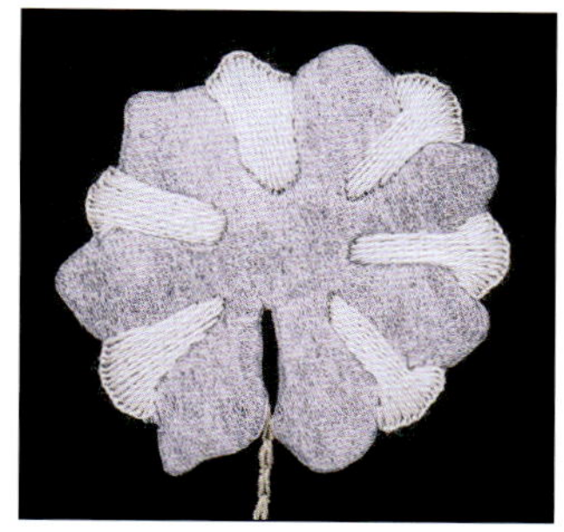

2. Using the lightest shade, J, work blanket stitch over the back petals.

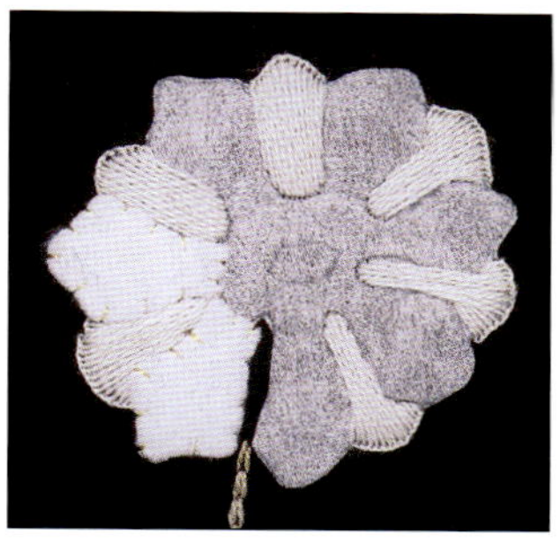

3. Padded petals. Cut out and attach the felt pieces with small stitches around the edges.

4. Work long and short blanket stitch to cover the felt shapes.

5. Add shading with straight stitches of varying lengths using B, C and E.

6. Highlight each petal with straight stitches using N. Work a straight stitch in the green yarn, F, between each petal.

7. Centre. Cut out and attach the small circle of felt. Cover with satin stitch using G and then P.

8. Work satin stitch over the outer section of the centre in G or H.

9. With P, outline the padded centre with back stitch and add straight stitch highlights.

10. Scatter French knots around the edge of the centre using M, Q and R.

11. Variation. Embroider detached blanket stitch around the edges of the felt padded petals.

12. Using B, embroider a bullion loop with 30 wraps between each pair of petals.

Hugs & Kisses

Cool, pure cotton waffle provides a wonderfully textured background for a colourful nursery design. A lush summer garden, overflowing with beautiful flowers, surrounds a sweet little bear. A flowering vine twines around the blanket and the edges are finished with piping and fine gingham fabric.

Requirements

Fabric

100cm x 83cm wide (40" x 33") piece of white cotton waffle weave

109cm x 92cm wide (43" x 36") piece of hot pink cotton gingham

10cm x 25cm wide (4" x 10") piece of hot pink cotton floral print

Supplies

15cm x 12cm wide (6" x 5") piece of natural coloured felt

15cm x 10mm wide (6" x 3/8") white cotton lace edging

20cm x 5mm wide (8" x 3/16") hot pink gingham ribbon

3.5m (3yd 30") strawberry pink mini piping

2 x 5mm (3/16") white buttons

Small amount of polyester fibre-fill

White tissue paper

Water-soluble fabric marker

Sharp HB pencil

This Design Uses

Appliqué, Back stitch
Blanket stitch, Bullion knot
Chain stitch, Detached chain
Fly stitch, French knot, Granitos
Outline stitch, Satin stitch
Stem stitch, Straight stitch

• • •

Threads & Needles

See page 36.

Preparation for Embroidery

See the pattern sheet for the embroidery designs.

Preparing the fabric

With wrong sides together, fold the white cotton in half across the width. While folded and using pale machine sewing thread, stitch a row of tacking along the fold line. Refold the fabric along its length. Tack along the fold line in the same manner.

Transferring the designs

Centre design

Using tissue paper and the pencil, trace the outline for the bear and the circles for the hollyhocks. Mark the centres of the agapanthus, daisy flowers and the hyacinths with a dot. Trace lines for the lavender flowers, the stems and leaves of the agapanthus and the lower leaves of the hollyhocks. Mark the position of each bee with a dot and trace the placement marks.

Pin the tracing onto the right side of the fabric, aligning the placement marks on the tracing with the tacking.

Using pale machine sewing thread and small tacking stitches, tack through the tissue paper and the fabric along the design lines.

The finished blanket measures 100cm x 83cm wide (40" x 33")

Most tacking threads marking the design can remain in the work permanently as the embroidery will cover them.

Lightly moisten the tissue paper with a damp sponge, wait a few seconds, then carefully remove the paper.

Border design

Trace the two corner designs onto tissue paper. Flip the tracings over and trace two more corners as mirror images of the originals.

Pin a tracing in each corner with the placement marks 5cm (2") in from the raw edges of the fabric. Tack through the tracings and remove the tissue paper as before.

Using the water-soluble fabric marker and with the photograph as a guide, draw the trailing vine along the sides between the corners.

Embroidery

See the pattern sheet for the bear template. Refer to the step-by-step instructions on page 38 for embroidering the bear and page 39 for stitching the hollyhock and the daisy flowers.

Use the milliner's needle for the bullion knots and the no. 5 crewel needle when stitching with the perlé thread. The no. 7 crewel needle is used for all other embroidery.

Order of work

Bear

Following the directions in the construction section, prepare the bear's sundress.

Attach the felt bear at the marked position, adding the sundress and ribbon.

Hollyhocks

Beginning at the base and working towards the tip, embroider the flowers with blanket stitch pinwheels around each marked circle. Add a French knot at the centre of each hollyhock flower.

For the buds at the tip, work four pink and four green French knots.

Work the leaves in detached chain. Decrease the size of the stitches as you work towards the tip.

Agapanthus

Work the flowers with fly stitches radiating from the centre. Add the green highlights with four or five straight stitches.

Stitch the stems and, using the same thread, embroider the leaves with rows of chain stitch. Work from the base to the tip.

Daisies

Embroider the flowers following the step-by-step instructions.

Work the leaves with detached chain. Use the darker thread towards the base of the plant and the lighter thread towards the top.

Lavender

Embroider each lavender flower with a bullion knot secured with a long anchoring stitch.

Add two straight stitches at the tip of the anchoring stitch. Surround the base of each fower with a fly stitch that has a long anchoring stitch for foliage.

Hyacinths

Beginning at the base with the darker shade of thread and grading to the lightest at the top, stitch the flowers with French knots.

Embroider the stems and leaves with straight stitch.

Blue flowers

Scatter French knots around the base of all the plants.

Work fly stitches with long anchoring stitches for the leaves and stems.

Bees

Embroider the body with a bullion knot. To achieve the striped effect, use three strands each of black and yellow threaded into the needle together. Work the pairs of wings with detached chain.

Border design

Work the main stems in outline or stem stitch. Embroider the small stems and leaves with straight stitch and detached chain stitch.

Embroider the dark pink flowers with a granitos for each of the three petals. Work two stitches for each granitos. Add French knot centres. Scatter French knots worked in the paler pink threads for the buds, nestling them among the leaves.

Construction

See page 129.

THREADS *and* NEEDLES

DMC no. 3 perlé cotton
A = 519 vy lt wedgewood
DMC no. 5 perlé cotton
B = 335 rose
C = 470 lt avocado green
D = 746 off-white
E = 818 baby pink
F = 3326 lt rose
G = 3348 lt yellow-green
(2 skeins)
House of Embroidery perlé thread
H = 6 golden privet
I = 18 hydrangea

Gumnut Yarns 'Stars' stranded silk
J = 297 dk lavender
Needle Necessities stranded variegated cotton
K = 199 dk avocado green
DMC stranded cotton
L = 470 lt avocado green
M = 721 med orange spice
N = 738 vy lt tan
O = 742 lt tangerine
P = 743 yellow
Q = 745 vy lt yellow
R = 844 ultra dk beaver grey
S = 3348 lt yellow-green
T = 3747 vy lt blue-violet
DMC stranded variegated cotton
U = 94 lt leaf green
Finca stranded variegated cotton
V = 9335 vy lt rose
W = 9395 rose
Needles
No. 1 milliner's needle
No. 5 crewel needle
No. 7 crewel needle

EMBROIDERY KEY

All embroidery is worked with one strand unless otherwise specified.

Bear

Outline = N (blanket stitch)

Features = N
(2 strands, back stitch)

Ear highlights = V
(2 strands, back stitch)

Eyes = R
(6 strands, French knot, 1 wrap)

Mouth = R
(2 strands, back stitch)

Nose = R (2 strands,
satin stitch, back stitch)

Hollyhocks

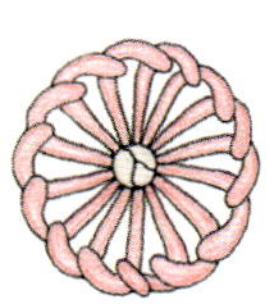

Flowers

Petals = V (6 strands,
blanket stitch)

Centre = D (French knot,
1 or 2 wraps)

Buds = V (6 strands, French
knot, 1 - 3 wraps) and K
(4 strands, French knot,
1 - 3 wraps)

Leaves = K
(4 strands, detached chain)

Agapanthus

Flowers

Petals = I (fly stitch)

Petal highlights = L
(2 strands, straight stitch)

Stems = C (outline stitch)

Leaves = C (chain stitch)

Daisies

Flowers

Petals = Q
(2 strands, granitos)

Petal outline = P (fly stitch)

Petal highlight = P (straight stitch)

Centre = M
(6 strands, French knot, 1 wrap)

Leaves = L and U
(6 strands, detached chain)

Lavender

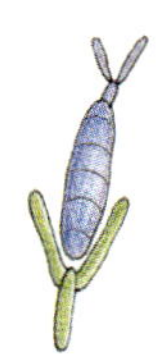

Flowers = J (6 strands,
bullion knot, 6 wraps,
1 strand, straight stitch)

Foliage = S
(3 strands, fly stitch)

Hyacinths

Flowers = W (6 strands,
French knot, 1 - 3 wraps)

Foliage = H (2 strands,
straight stitch)

Blue flowers

Flowers = A
(French knot, 1 wrap)

Foliage = H (fly stitch)

Bees

Body = P and R
(3 strands of each,
bullion knot, 3 wraps)

Wings = T (detached chain)

Border

Main stems = G
(outline or stem stitch)

Stems = S (straight stitch)

Leaves = G and S
(detached chain, straight stitch)

Dark pink flowers = B
(granitos)

Centre = O (2 strands,
French knot, 1 wrap)

Pale pink buds = E or F
(French knot, 1 wrap)

Embroidering *the* Bear

Cut out and prepare the bear's sundress following the directions on page 129.

1. Using the template, cut the bear from the felt. Pin the bear onto the fabric at the marked position.

2. Beginning and ending under the arms, work blanket stitch around the body and the legs.

3. Evenly fill the legs and tummy with fibre-fill.

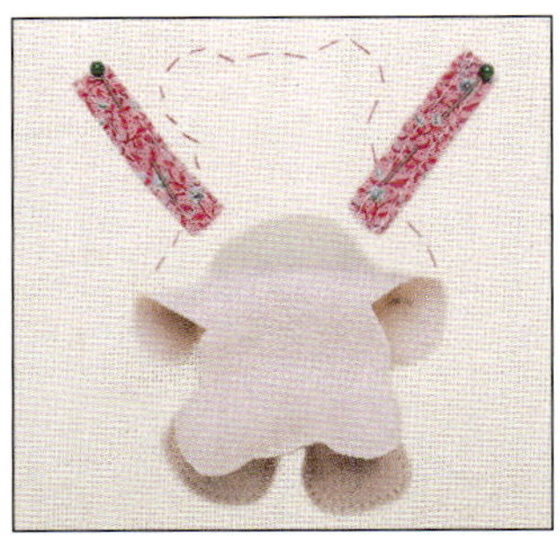

4. Pin the shoulder straps onto the marked design with 6mm (1/4") extending into the marked bear shape.

5. Reposition the upper section of the bear.

6. From the marked points on the ears, blanket stitch down the sides of the head and arms. Stitch through the straps.

7. Fold the straps down into position. Place the sundress over the straps and secure with buttons.

8. Pin the paws over the sides of the dress. Complete the blanket stitching around the paws and arms.

9. Evenly fill the arms and head with fibre-fill.

10. Complete the blanket stitching across the ears and head.

11. Working through the padded layers, back stitch the shaping within the head and body.

12. Work the eyes, nose and mouth through the padded layers. Pull the stitches firmly to mould the face.

13. Tie the ribbon in a small bow. Attach firmly to the top of the head. Fold under the tails and hand stitch just below the ears.

HOLLYHOCK

Often called blanket stitch pinwheels, these pretty flowers are formed from blanket stitches worked in a circle. This method of stitching a flower is particularly suitable for working these graceful spires of hollyhocks. We have used perlé thread for photographic purposes.

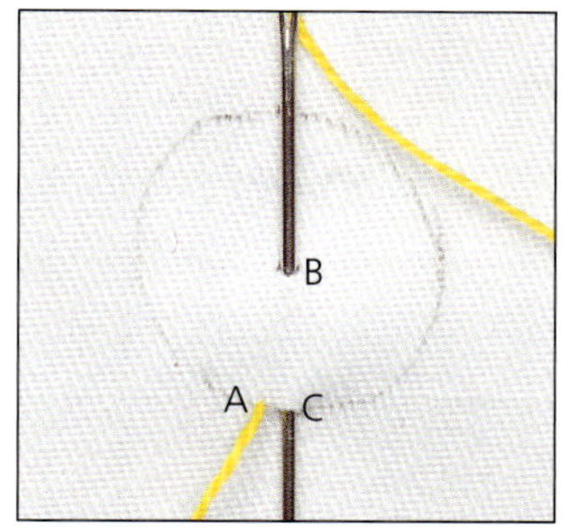

1. Draw a circle and mark the centre. Bring the thread to the front at A. Take the needle from B to C just to the right of A.

2. Place the thread under the needle tip. Begin to pull the thread through, pulling away from the circle.

3. Pull until loop sits on circle. With thread under needle tip, take needle from centre to edge of circle, just right of previous stitch.

4. Continue working stitches around the circle, turning the fabric as you work.

5. For the last stitch, take the needle from the centre to A. With thread under needle, pull through. Take the needle to back just over loop.

6. Pull the thread through. End off on the back. Work a French knot in the centre to complete the flower.

DAISY

To achieve an even placement of stitches, work the first three petals in a Y shape, then fill in the spaces with the final two petals.

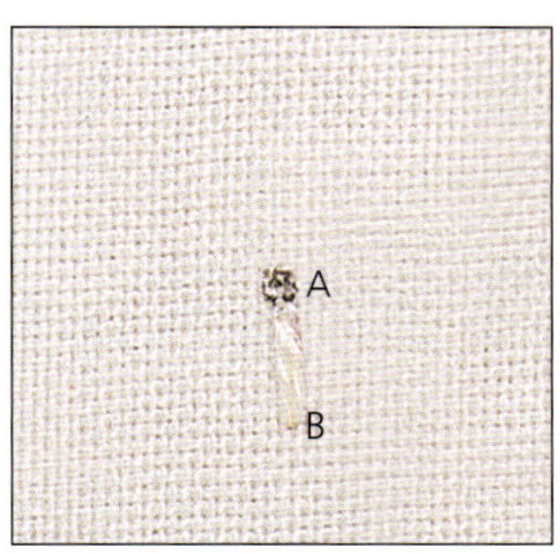

1. Petal. Bring the thread to the front at the centre, A. Take to the back at B and pull through.

2. Work two more stitches using the same two holes. Gently pull through, with the stitches side by side.

3. Work four more granitos petals in the order indicated on the photo. Place them evenly around the centre.

4. Petal outline. Bring new thread to front at C. With thread below, take needle to back at D. Emerge at E.

5. Holding the loop, pull the thread through until the loop lies snugly against E.

6. Take the thread to the back at F to anchor. Add a straight stitch highlight. Repeat for each petal.

7. Centre. Using a new thread, work a French knot at the centre.

A
B
C

A
B
C

Cascading ribbons and delicate clusters of roses form a wonderful border on this dainty nursery blanket. Alphabet blocks and a cuddly bear and bunny are stitched in a combination of gentle pastel threads on creamy pure wool flannel. The beautifully shaped edges are finished with baby pink piping and the blanket is backed with soft ivory twill.

Requirements

Fabric

102cm x 74cm wide (40" x 29") piece of ivory doctor's flannel

102cm x 74cm wide (40" x 29") piece of ivory polycotton twill

Supplies

102cm x 74cm wide (40" x 29") piece of thin wadding

15cm x 20cm wide (6" x 8") piece of white felt

3.3m (3yd 22") baby pink piping made using size 1 piping cord

Small amount of polyester fibre-fill

15cm (6") embroidery hoop

White tissue paper

Sharp HB lead pencil

Chalk based fabric marker

This Design Uses

Back stitch, Bullion knot
Bullion loop, Couching
Detached chain, French knot
Long and short stitch
Straight stitch
Whipped back stitch

• • •

Threads & Needles

See page 46.

Preparation for Embroidery

See page 129 for preparing the fabric and the pattern sheet for the embroidery designs.

Stitch tension is very important as stitches that are pulled too tightly will pucker the fabric. Stitch with a slightly looser tension than you would with cotton or silk thread.

After embroidering the ribbons and blocks, press on the back with a steam iron. Alternatively, mist the fabric with water and press with a dry iron.

THE FINISHED BLANKET MEASURES 100CM X 72CM WIDE (39" X 28")

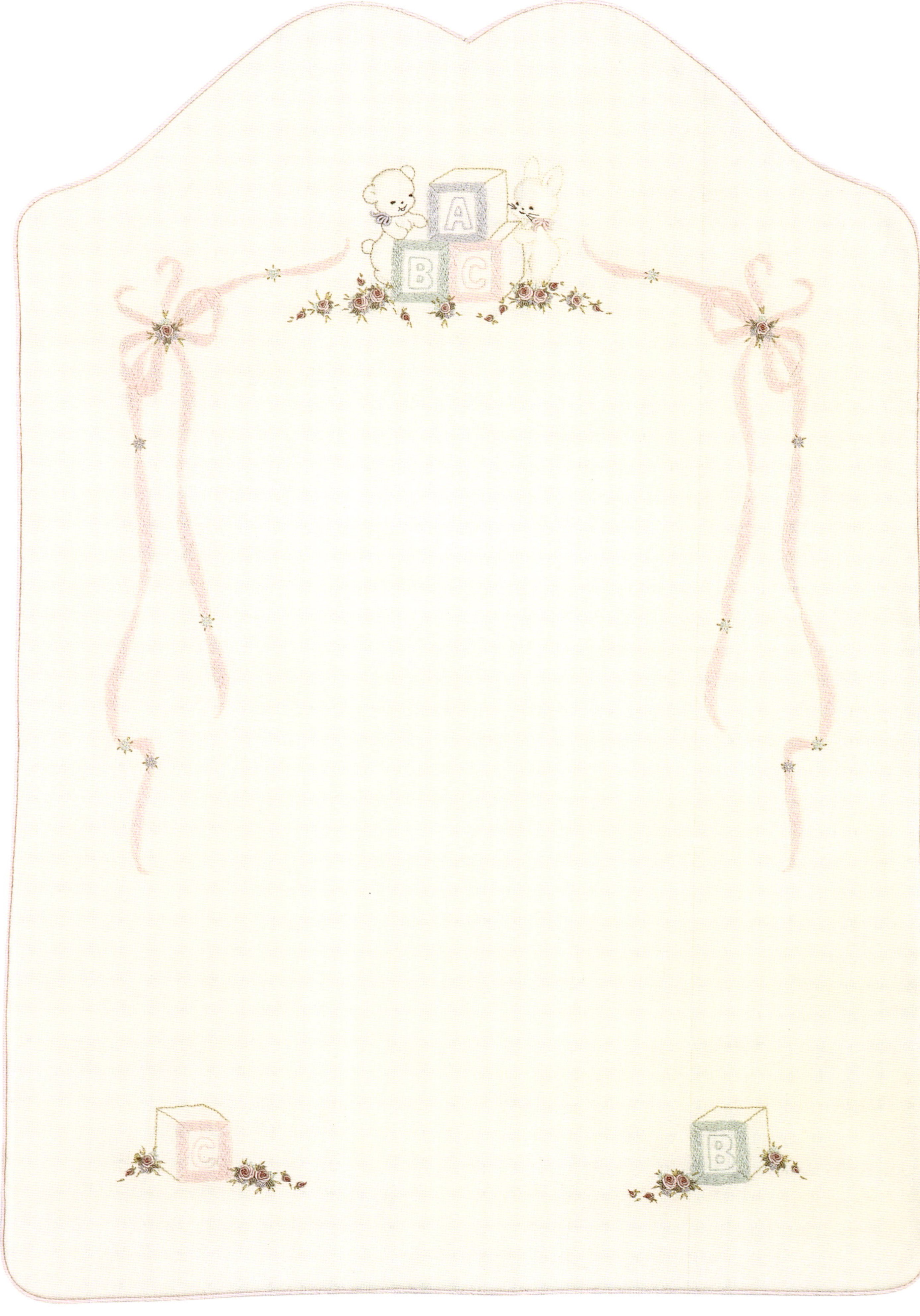

Transferring the designs

Using the pencil, trace the main embroidery design and placement marks onto tissue paper. Repeat for the bows and lower corner designs.

Place the tracing of the main design over the upper section of the flannel, matching the placement marks with the tacking. Pin the tissue in place to prevent movement. Using pale machine sewing thread and small stitches, tack through the tissue paper and the doctor's flannel along the design lines. Mark the centre of each rose with a small cross stitch. Most stitches can remain in the work permanently as the embroidery will cover them.

Lightly moisten the tissue paper with a damp sponge. Wait a few seconds, then carefully remove the paper, leaving the stitches behind.

Transfer a bow design to each side of the flannel and the corner designs to the lower edge in the same manner as the main design.

EMBROIDERY

See the step-by-step instructions on page 48 for working the padded bunny and page 49 for whipped back stitch.

Use the tapestry needle for all wool embroidery and when working the whipping on the alphabet blocks. The no. 1 milliner's needle is used for the bullion roses, the no. 9 milliner's needle for bullion leaves and daisies and the crewel needle for all other embroidery.

Place the fabric in the embroidery hoop for all embroidery except the flowers.

Order of work

Bunny

Cut the piece of felt in half. Using one piece and referring to the step-by-step instructions, stitch the bunny.

Bear

Using the remaining piece of felt, work the bear in the same manner as the bunny.

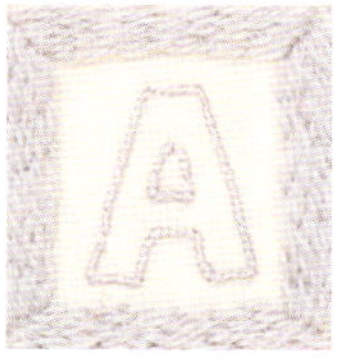

Alphabet blocks

Outline the side and back of each block in back stitch. Fill the border on the front of each block with long and short stitch. When embroidering the blocks next to the bunny and bear, work the stitches through the flannel and felt layers.

Work the letters in whipped back stitch referring to the step-by-step instructions.

Bows

Embroider long and short stitch along the bows and ribbons, referring to the photograph for stitch direction.

Roses

Using the darkest shade of pink, work one or two bullion knots for the centre of each rose. Change to the medium shade for the inner petals and the lightest shade for the outer petals. Add leaves around the roses. For each, work two bullion knots, securing one with a long anchoring stitch.

Buds

Using the darkest shade of pink, stitch the centre of each bud with one or two bullion knots, securing one with a longer anchoring stitch. Add the petals with the medium shade. Stitch the calyx with one bullion knot on each side at the base.

Daisies

Work the partial violet daisies among the roses with two to four pairs of bullion knots. Stitch the violet daisies on the ribbon tails with five pairs of bullion knots. Add a French knot centre.

For the partial blue-green daisies among the roses, work three or four detached chain petals. Work the blue-green daisies on the ribbon tails with six detached chain petals. Add a French knot centre.

Leaves

Using the photograph as a guide, scatter detached chain leaves around the sprays and individual flowers.

CONSTRUCTION

See pages 129 and 130.

THREADS *and* NEEDLES

DMC stranded cotton

A = 223 lt shell pink
B = 224 vy lt shell pink
C = 225 ultra lt shell pink
D = 370 med verdigris
E = 504 vy lt blue-green
F = 677 vy lt old gold
G = 844 ultra dk beaver grey
H = 3023 lt Jacobean green
I = 3743 vy lt antique violet

Appleton 2 ply crewel wool

J = 691 ultra lt honeysuckle yellow
K = 882 ecru
L = 981 lt putty groundings

Paterna Persian yarn

M = D147 lt basil
N = 524 lt teal blue
O = 935 vy lt rusty rose (2 skeins)

Needles

No. 1 milliner's needle
No. 9 milliner's needle
No. 9 crewel needle
No. 24 tapestry needle

EMBROIDERY KEY

All embroidery is worked with one strand unless otherwise specified.

Bunny

Outline = K (back stitch)
Ear marking = O (back stitch)
Face = G (straight stitch)
Bow loops = C (6 strands, bullion loop, 30 wraps), C (couching)
Bow tails = C (6 strands, bullion knot, 20 wraps), C (couching)
Bow knot = C (6 strands, straight stitch)

Bear

Outline = L (back stitch)
Ear marking = L (back stitch)
Face = G (straight stitch)
Bow loops = I (6 strands, bullion loop, 30 wraps), I (couching)
Bow tails = I (6 strands, bullion knot, 20 wraps), I (couching)
Bow knot = I (6 strands, straight stitch)

Alphabet blocks

A block

Outline = J (back stitch)
Border = M (long and short stitch)
Letter = I (2 strands, whipped back stitch)

B blocks

Outline = J (back stitch)
Border = N (long and short stitch)
Letter = E (2 strands, whipped back stitch)

C blocks

Outline = J (back stitch)
Border = O (long and short stitch)
Letter = C (2 strands, whipped back stitch)

Bows = O (long and short stitch)

Roses

Centre = A (3 strands, 1 or 2 bullion knots, 10 - 12 wraps)
Inner petals = B (3 strands, 2 or 3 bullion knots, 15 - 20 wraps)
Outer petals = C (3 strands, 2 to 6 bullion knots, 15 - 20 wraps)
Leaves = H (2 bullion knots, 10 - 20 wraps)

Buds

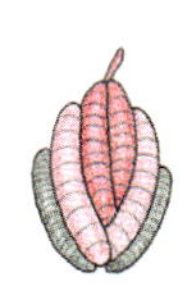

Centre = A (3 strands, 1 or 2 bullion knots, 10 - 12 wraps)
Petals = B (3 strands, 2 bullion knots, 10 - 15 wraps)
Calyx = H (2 bullion knots, 15 - 20 wraps)

Violet daisies

Petals = I (bullion knot, 12 wraps)
Centre = F (2 strands, French knot, 1 wrap)
Leaves = D (detached chain)

Blue-green daisies

Petals = E (2 strands, detached chain)
Centre = F (2 strands, French knot, 1 wrap)
Leaves = D (detached chain)

Scattered leaves = D (detached chain)

You can make this blanket using an alternate colourway, by replacing the pink with blue for the blocks, ribbons and the piping.

A
B
C

B

C

Stitching the Bunny

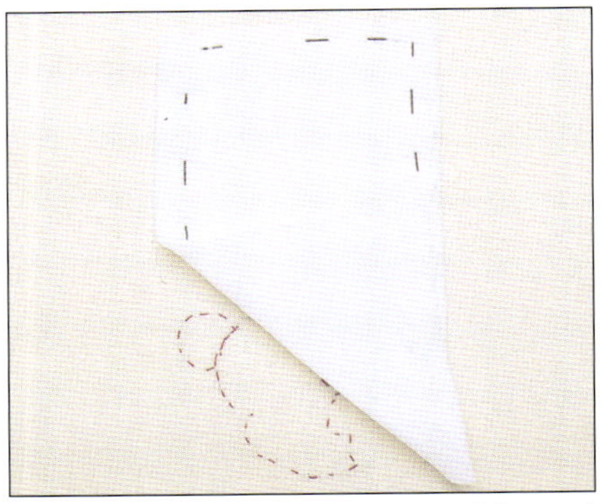

1. Place felt onto wrong side of flannel so it extends just beyond the tacked outline of the bunny. Tack.

2. On right side, back stitch around head and ears leaving an opening at the neck. Leave thread dangling.

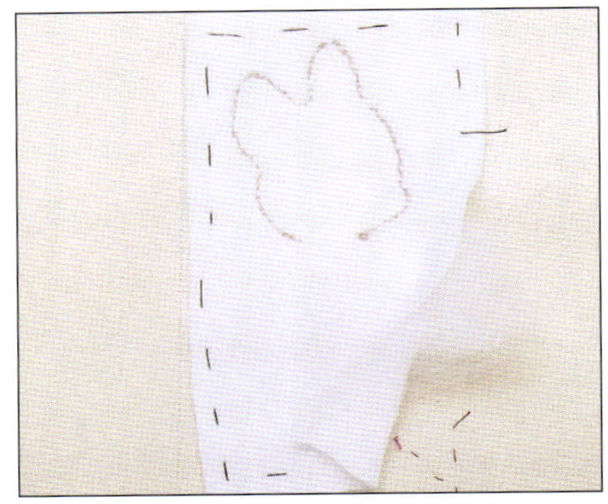

3. Unpick some tacking from the felt. Working through opening, evenly fill head and ears with fibre-fill.

4. On the right side, back stitch the neck opening closed using the dangling thread.

5. Leaving an opening at the tummy, stitch around the outline for the body, arm, leg and tail.

6. Fill evenly with the fibre-fill as before. Close the opening with a temporary row of tacking.

7. Working through the padded layers, back stitch the internal design lines.

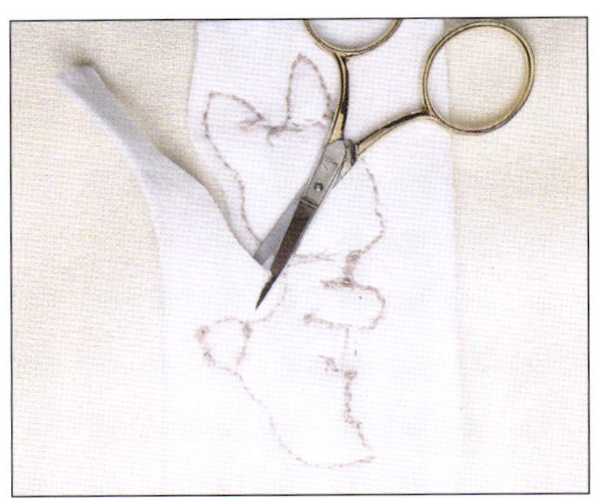

8. On the back, trim the felt away close to the bunny outline.

9. Work the eyes and nose through the padded layers, pulling the straight stitches firmly to mould the face.

10. Stitch the mouth and whiskers in straight stitch, skimming the stitches behind the flannel layer only.

11. Work the bow loops and tails and couch in place.

12. Embroider the side of the alphabet block to secure the opening. Remove the tacking as necessary.

Whipped Back Stitch

Whipped back stitch is worked in two stages and has a raised, corded appearance. Use a tapestry needle for the whipping and keep the tension of the stitches loose but even.

We have used contrasting thread for photographic purposes.

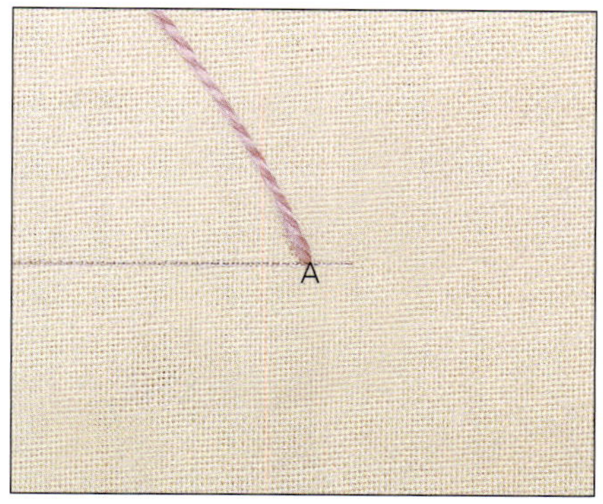

1. Foundation. Bring thread to front at A, 1.5mm (1/16") from the start of the marked line.

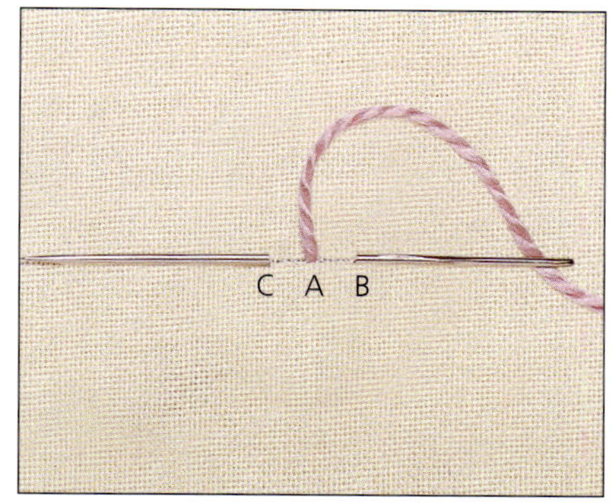

2. Take the needle to the back at B at the start of the line. Emerge at C, 1.5mm (1/16") beyond A.

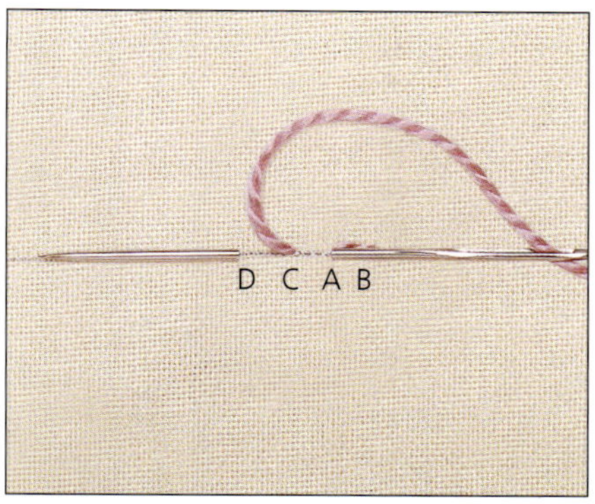

3. Pull thread through. Take the needle to the back at A, through the same hole, and emerge at D.

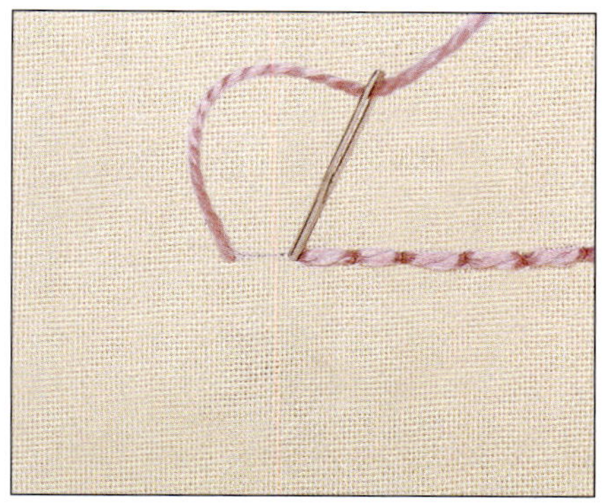

4. Continue along the row. To end off, take the needle through the hole at the beginning of the previous stitch.

5. Whipping. Bring thread to the front just below the centre of the back stitch at one end.

6. Slide the needle from top to bottom under the next back stitch. Do not pick up any fabric.

7. Pull thread through, using a loose tension. Slide the needle from top to bottom under the next back stitch.

8. Continue along the row. To end off, take the needle to the back under the centre of the last stitch.

Hints on Using and Caring for Blankets

Our blankets are not just decorative - they are designed to be used, either on a bed or as a wrap or throw. If using a blanket in a cot, remember to tuck it in firmly and to keep it away from the baby's face.

To care for your blanket, either have it dry cleaned or gently handwash it in warm water using a mild soap or detergent. Squeeze as much excess moisture as you can before hanging or laying it out to dry.

Wool blanketing and doctor's flannel are largely made from natural fibres and so need to be able to breathe. When storing blankets ensure they are perfectly clean and away from strong light. Never place them in plastic.

Add a little magic to your world with this lovable duckling sitting in the midst of a flower patch of daisies and violets. The colourful creature clasps a resplendent daisy and is surrounded by bees and butterflies.

Requirements

Fabric

114cm x 75cm wide (45" x 30") piece of lilac wool blanketing

132cm x 93cm wide (52" x 37") piece of cotton check

20cm (8") square of yellow homespun

Supplies

Small amount of polyester fibre-fill

3.3m (3yd 22") pale lilac mini piping

White tissue paper

Sharp HB pencil

Threads & Needles

See page 56.

This Design Uses

Appliqué, Back stitch
Bullion knot, Couching
Detached chain, French knot
Ghiordes knot, Ladder stitch
Long and short stitch
Padded satin stitch
Pistil stitch, Running stitch
Straight stitch

Preparation for Embroidery

See page 130 for preparing the fabrics and the pattern sheet for the embroidery design and the feet and beak templates.

Transferring the design

Trace the embroidery design, including the placement marks, onto the tissue paper. Position the tracing on the right side of the blanketing, aligning the placement marks with the lines of tacking. Pin the tracing in place.

Using pale machine sewing thread and small tacking stitches, tack through the tissue paper and the blanketing along the design lines.

Most tacking threads marking the design can remain in the work permanently as the embroidery will cover them.

Lightly moisten the tissue paper with a damp sponge, wait a few seconds, then carefully remove the paper.

THE FINISHED BLANKET MEASURES 114CM X 75CM WIDE (45" X 30")

EMBROIDERY

See the step-by-step instructions on pages 56 and 57 for making the twisted cord stem and page 57 for working a butterfly.

Use the no. 22 chenille needle for stitching with the wool and the no. 18 chenille needle for anchoring the twisted cord. Work the bullion knots and French knots using the no. 5 milliner's needle. Use the no. 9 crewel needle for one or two strands of cotton or metallic thread and the no. 5 crewel needle for all other embroidery.

Order of work

Duckling

Beak and feet

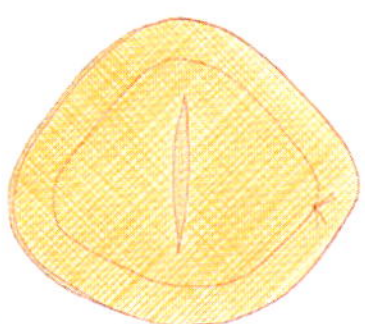

Diag 1

With right sides together, pin and stitch the two beak pieces along the stitch line. Cut a small slit in the back *(diag 1)*. Turn to the right side and fill with a small amount of fibre-fill. Hand stitch the small opening closed. Construct the feet in the same manner. Using matching sewing thread, attach the beak and feet to the blanketing with ladder stitch *(diag 2)*.

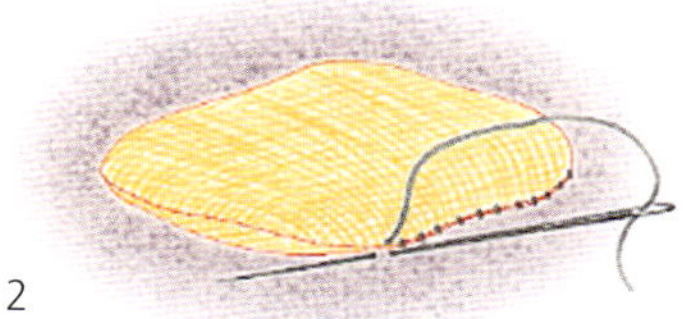

Diag 2

Work back stitch through the two layers of homespun and the blanketing along the marked lines to sculpt the beak.

Head

Starting with the darker shade of yellow wool, work long and short stitch from the beak outwards. Vary the length of the stitches. Stitch over the top of this with the lighter shade and then, less densely, with the stranded cottons.

Eyes

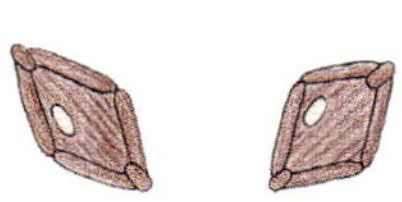

Diag 3

Embroider the eyes with padded satin stitch. Work two fly stitches cupping each eye and add the ecru highlights *(diag 3)*.

Body and wings

Referring to the photograph for stitch direction, embroider the body and wings in the same manner as the head. Outline the wings.

Garden

Grass

Using the three green wools, work straight stitch in varying lengths for the grass.

Tiny flowers

Scatter French knots among the grass.

Violets

Diag 4

Embroider the violets with one upper petal and three lower petals. Work French knots for the centres *(diag 4)*. Work the stems, then add the leaves.

Forget-me-nots

Embroider the five petals and the contrasting centre with French knots. Add the stems and leaves.

Daisy

Following the step-by-step instructions, make the twisted cord stem from the mohair. Lay the cord between the placement for the flower and the wings of the duck. Attach with three couching stitches *(diag 5)*. Take the end of the cord to the back at the base of the flower and fasten securely. With the other end, take a stitch under the wing, then take the cord to the back at the base of the duck. Finish off as before.

Diag 5

Embroider the straight stitch petals with the ecru wool and rayon. Work five French knots for the centre.

Butterflies

Embroider the butterflies following the step-by-step instructions.

Bees

Work five bullion knots for the body. Begin with the central yellow stripe using ten wraps. Work a brown stripe on each side, using nine wraps. Add a yellow bullion knot of seven or eight wraps at each end.

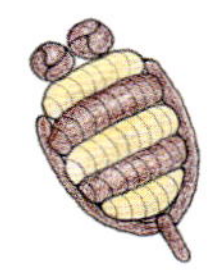

Diag 6

Work a fly stitch around the body, anchoring it at the tail to form the stinger. Add two French knots for the eyes *(diag 6)*.

Embroider two blended blue and black-gold Ghiordes knots on each side of the body for wings.

Add the flight path of the bees in running stitch.

CONSTRUCTION

See page 130.

Metallic thread can be difficult to work with because it breaks easily. Use short lengths to make it more manageable and to maintain its quality.

As the section of thread in the eye of the needle wears quickly, adjust frequently or tie the tail of thread to the eye of the needle.

~ Threads *and* Needles ~

Anchor stranded cotton
A = 98 lavender
B = 120 lt periwinkle blue
C = 121 periwinkle blue
D = 122 dk periwinkle blue
E = 292 vy lt golden yellow
F = 301 butter yellow
G = 302 lt pumpkin
H = 303 pumpkin
I = 311 straw
J = 360 chocolate
K = 379 mocha
Anchor Marlitt rayon
L = 895 ultra vy lt pine green
M = 1212 cream
Paterna Persian yarn
N = 602 forest green
O = 703 lt butterscotch
P = 704 vy lt butterscotch
Mogear 100% mohair
Q = 39 olive
R = 39a olive tree
Appleton 2 ply crewel wool
S = 696
dk honeysuckle yellow
T = 882 ecru
U = 955 med drab fawn
Madeira FS no. 15 metallic thread
V = 22 gold
Minnamurra variegated stranded cotton
W = 110 violet/gold
Au Papillon Fil d'Or de Luxe
X = black-gold
Kreinik Metallics blending filament
Y = 042 confetti fuchsia
Au Ver á Soie, Soie d'Alger stranded silk
Z = 1835 green
Needles
No. 5 crewel needle
No. 9 crewel needle
No. 5 milliner's needle
No. 18 chenille needle
No. 22 chenille needle

~ Embroidery Key ~

All embroidery is worked with one strand unless otherwise specified.

Duck
Beak and feet = G (back stitch)
Head, body and wings = O and P (long and short stitch), G and I (2 strands, long and short stitch)
Eyes = J (4 strands, padded satin stitch, fly stitch), T (straight stitch)
Wing outline = S (back stitch)

Garden
Grass = N, Q and R (straight stitch)
Tiny flowers = D and E (6 strands, French knot, 1 wrap), A and W (4 strands, French knot, 1 wrap)

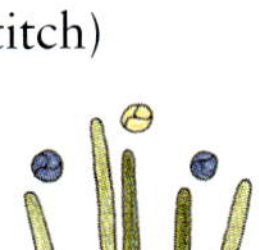

Violets
Petals = A (2 strands, detached chain)
Centre = H (3 strands, French knot, 1 wrap)
Stems and leaves = L (straight stitch, detached chain)

Forget-me-nots
Petals = C (3 strands, French knot, 1 wrap)

Centre = F (3 strands, French knot, 1 wrap)
Stems and leaves = Z (straight stitch, detached chain)

Daisy
Stem = Q (twisted cord, couching)
Petals = M (4 strands, straight stitch), T (straight stitch)
Centre = E (6 strands, French knot, 1 wrap)

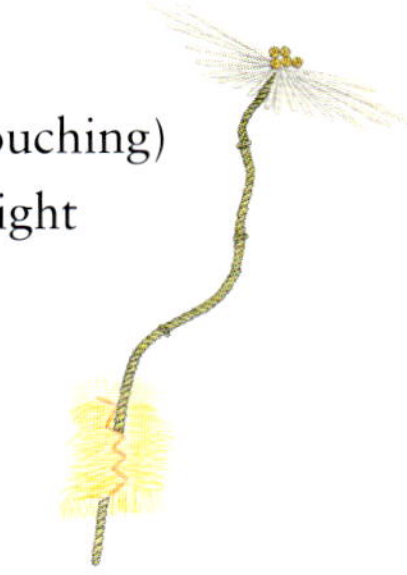

Butterflies
Wings = 1 strand of V blended with 2 strands of Y (Ghiordes knot, detached chain)
Body = K (4 strands, bullion knot, 10 - 12 wraps)
Head = K (4 strands, French knot, 1 wrap)
Antennae = V (pistil stitch)

Bees
Body = I and J (4 strands, bullion knot, 7 - 10 wraps), J (fly stitch)
Eyes = J (4 strands, French knot, 1 wrap)
Wings = B and X (1 strand of each blended, Ghiordes knot)
Flight path = X (running stitch)

~ *Step-by-Step* ~

Making the Twisted Cord

A twisted cord is used for the stem of the daisy. The cord is made with mohair. We used a tool called a spinster to make our twisted cord.

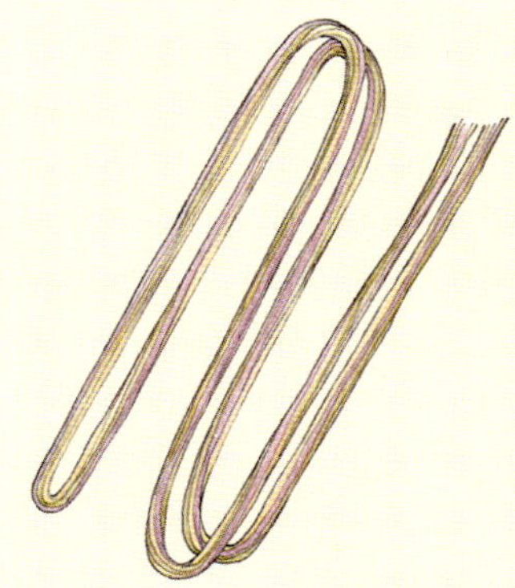

1. Cut one strand of mohair measuring 125cm (50") long. Fold in half to give two strands.

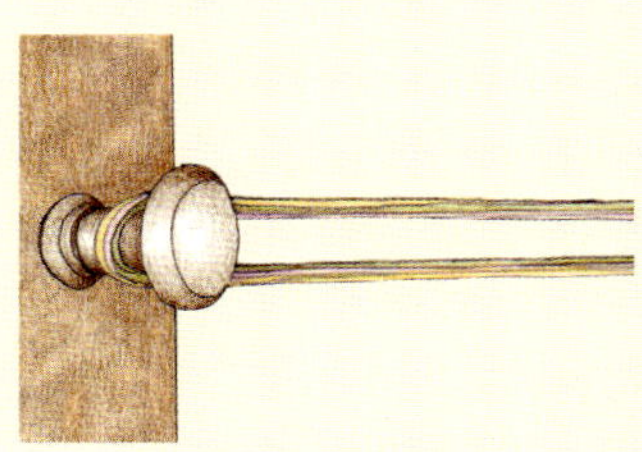

2. Knot the ends together and hook the loop of the folded end over a door handle.

3. Hook the knotted end onto the hook of the spinster.

4. Keeping threads taut, turn them in a clockwise direction until the twist has the desired tension.

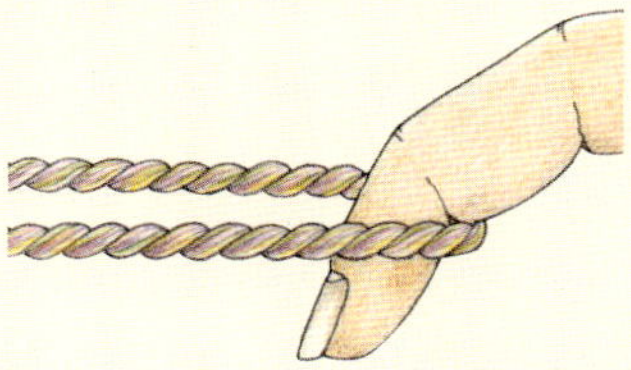

5. Bring the two ends together, holding at the halfway point.

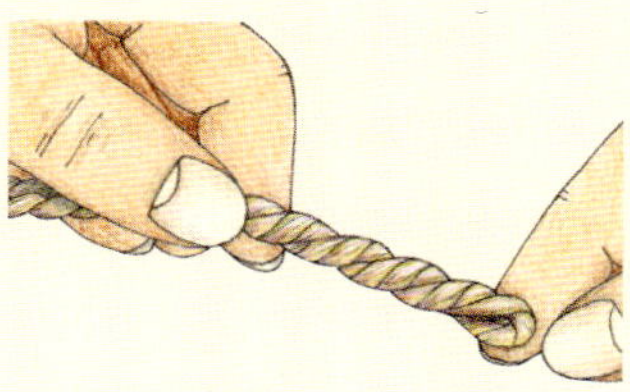

6. Keeping twisted threads fully stretched, release 10-15cm (4-6") at a time until all the cord is twisted.

7. Remove the loop from the door knob and knot the ends together.

BUTTERFLY

The butterfly above the daisy is worked following these step-by-step instructions, while the butterfly on the left is worked as a mirror image.

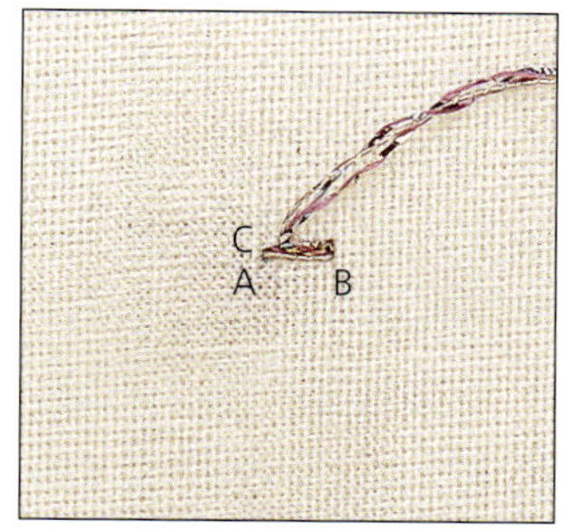

1. **Front wings.** Bring thread to front at A. Take thread to back at B and emerge at C. Pull thread through.

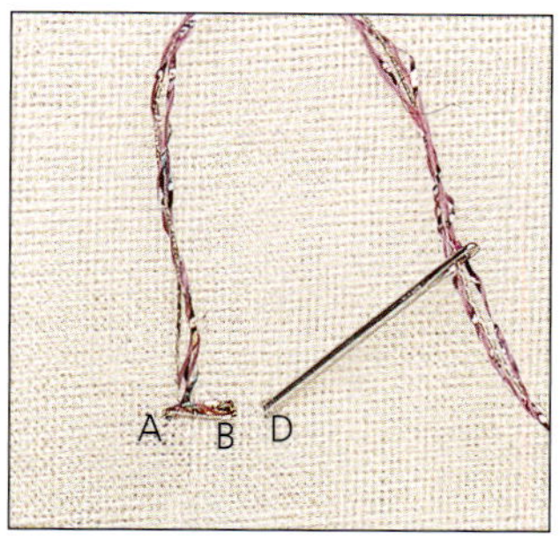

2. With the thread above, take the needle to the back at D, ready to form a loop.

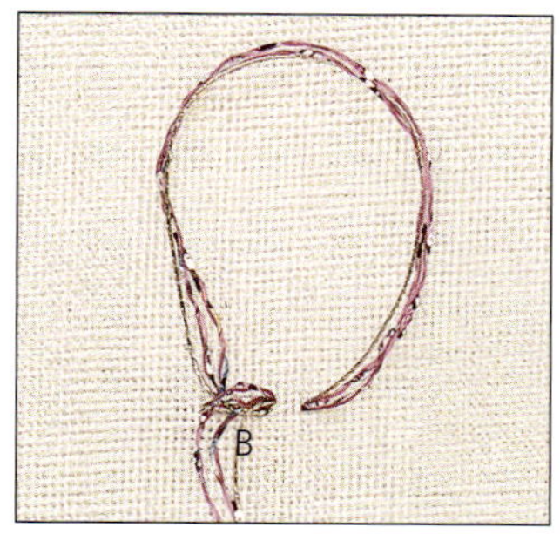

3. Pull thread through. Holding the loop flat on the fabric, bring the needle to the front at B.

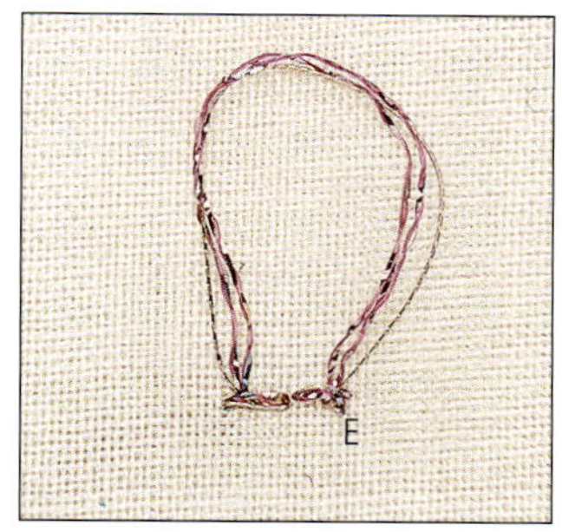

4. With thread below, take needle to the back at E. Pull thread through to form a back stitch.

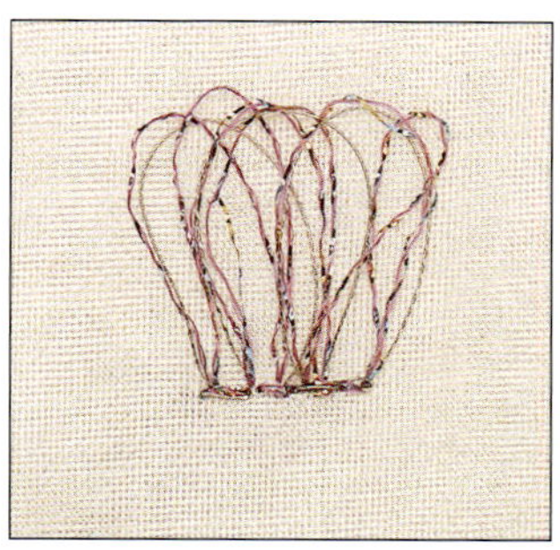

5. Work two more loops finishing with the thread at the back.

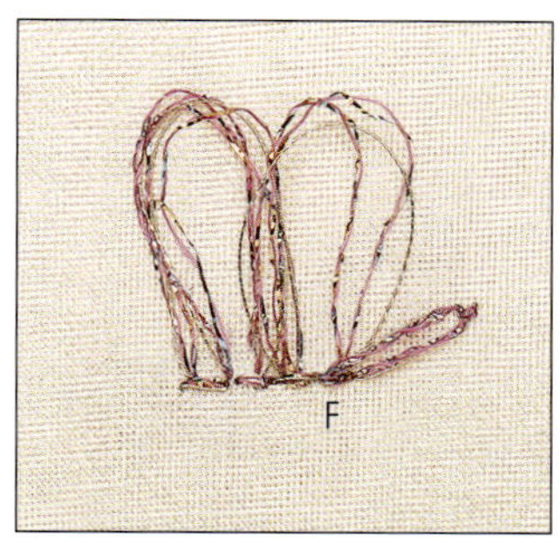

6. **Back wings.** Bring thread to the front at F and work a detached chain.

7. Work a slightly longer detached chain around the first stitch.

8. **Body.** At the base of the wings, work a 10 - 12 wrap bullion knot.

9. **Head.** With same thread, work a French knot at the front of the body.

10. **Antennae.** Work two pistil stitches near the top of the head.

A superb oval wreath, *bursting with wild roses, berries and Queen Anne's lace, forms the centrepiece of this luxurious blanket. Embroidered over a delicate pink ribbon bow, the magnificent central design is echoed in each corner. Dainty posies of bullion roses and gypsophila, tied with blue silk ribbon, are nestled in the wreath and between the large corner sprays. The blanket is backed with a pretty floral print and the edges are bound with rich cream satin.*

REQUIREMENTS

Fabric

1.2m x 150cm wide (1yd 12" x 59") ivory doctor's flannel

1.5m x 120cm wide (1yd 23" x 48") floral cotton print

1.6m x 60cm wide (1yd 27" x 24") piece of cream duchess satin

Supplies

1.5m x 120cm wide (1yd 23" x 48") piece of thin wadding

36cm (14") quilting hoop

Tracing paper

Tissue paper

Sharp HB pencil

Fine black permanent pen

Threads, Ribbons, Beads & Needles

See page 69.

THIS DESIGN USES

Appliqué, Back stitch, Beading
Bullion knot, Couching
Fly stitch, French knot
Grab stitch
Long and short stitch
Running stitch, Stem stitch
Straight stitch
Twisted ribbon stitch

PREPARATION FOR EMBROIDERY

See page 131 for preparing the fabric and the pattern sheet for the embroidery designs.

Transferring the design

Pink bow

Trace the ribbon appliqué for the wreath design, including placement marks, onto tissue paper with the pencil. Pin the tracing onto the doctor's flannel, matching placement marks with the lines of tacking.

Using machine sewing thread, tack along the design lines for the large bow loops and ties.

Lightly moisten the tissue paper with a damp sponge, wait a few seconds, then carefully remove the paper.

by HELEN ERIKSSON

The finished blanket measures 150cm x 120cm wide (59" x 48")

Cut the pink ribbon in half. Using one piece, pin the midpoint to the marked position on the fabric.

Working with one half of the ribbon, form a bow loop and tails to correspond with the tacking lines. With the tail beneath the loop, pin the loop in place.

Repeat with the other end of the same piece of ribbon. Tack in place *(diag 1)*.

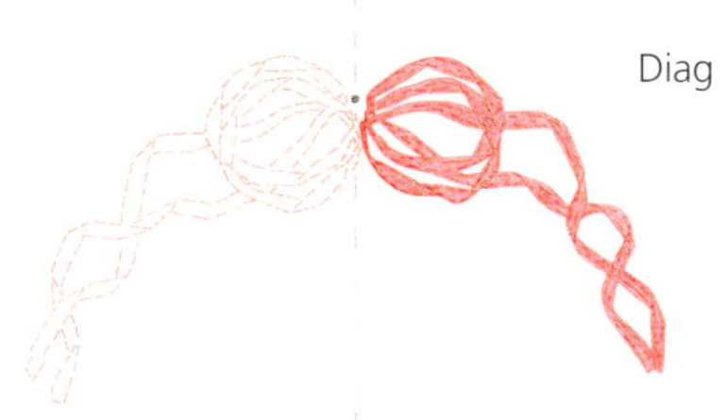

Form the remaining half of the bow and tails with the other ribbon piece.

Using very small running stitches on the front and slightly larger ones on the back of the work, stitch along the satin edges of the ribbon.

Remove the bow tacking stitches.

Wreath, corner designs and bouquets

Trace the embroidery designs onto the tracing paper using the black pen. Place the wreath tracing beneath the fabric. Using a light box or window, align the placement marks with the lines of tacking. Pin in place. Lightly trace the design with the pencil, drawing over the ribbon appliqué where necessary.

Referring to the photograph, transfer the corner designs in a similar manner, then the bouquets, placing one between each corner.

Embroidery

Refer to pages 70 and 71 for the step-by-step instructions for working the berry, the blue flower spray and the blue bow.

All embroidery is worked with the fabric in the hoop.

Use the no. 9 milliner's needle for working the centres of the wild rose blossoms and for attaching the beads. The no. 3 milliner's needle is used for the bullion knot buds and the sepals on the berries, gypsophila and Queen Anne's lace.

The no. 1 milliner's needle is used for the bullion knot roses and the berries. Use the no. 18 chenille needle when stitching the wild rose blossoms, buds and leaves and the blue sprays. For the silk ribbon bows and remaining wool stems and leaves, stitch with the no. 22 chenille needle. The crewel needle is used for all remaining embroidery.

Order of work

The wreath consists of four wild rose sprays and four rose bouquets. Work the flowers over the pink ribbon.

Wild rose sprays

Wild rose

Following the photograph for colour placement, embroider the petals of the wild rose blossoms first. Work the highlights over the petals.

Fill in the centres with tightly packed French knots using the three shades of green thread.

For the two side view blossoms, work a calyx at the base with a fly stitch. Fill the fly stitch with tiny straight stitches. Work the stems in stem stitch.

Embroider the petals for the blossom buds in the same colours as the flowers. Stitch each calyx in shades of green. Work straight stitch along the outer edges of some. Add three to five straight stitches or fly stitches to the tips of the buds. Where the base is visible, work a grab stitch, finishing some with a long anchoring stitch. Continue in the same thread and work the remainder of each stem in stem stitch. Embroider the tiny leaves in straight stitch.

Starting at the tip, work the large leaves in long and short stitch. Using the rayon thread, work the central veins in stem stitch. Add side veins in straight stitch to some. Embroider straight stitch along the outer edges of most leaves, forming a broken outline.

CENTRAL WREATH

Berries

Referring to the step-by-step instructions and using the photograph as a guide for colour placement, work the berries.

Embroider the stems in stem stitch adding straight stitch leaves.

Bullion roses

Embroider the roses with three bullion knots for the centres. Work five or six bullion knots for the inner petals and six to eight bullion knots for the outer petals.

Starting at the tip, embroider the tiny curved leaves for the roses in fly stitch, keeping the stitches close together.

Gypsophila

Work the stems in fly stitch with long anchoring stitches and straight stitch.

Embroider the flowers along the fly stitch branches with French knots.

Queen Anne's lace

Stitch the stems in stem stitch and the bracts with straight stitch. Couch along the straight stitches so the bracts form slight curves. Work each flower with five to seven French knot petals and add a tiny bead for each centre.

Blue sprays

Embroider the stems and buds following the step-by-step instructions.

Rose and gypsophila bouquets

Embroider the three large roses and leaves in a similar manner as before. Stitch the inner petals with six bullion knots. Work the outer petals with seven or eight bullion knots. Embroider the stems for the roses and leaves in stem stitch.

Stitch the four large buds with two bullion knots for each centre and a bullion knot at each side for the petals. Embroider two fly stitches for the calyx and a straight stitch along the centre of each bud. Work two or three straight stitches at the tip of most buds.

Embroider the two small buds in the same manner as the large buds, omitting the two outer petals. Stitch the stems for the buds in stem stitch or back stitch.

The stems for the gypsophila are embroidered in the same manner as before, adding tiny beads along the stems for the flowers.

Blue bow

Cut a 30cm (12") length of the blue silk ribbon for each bow. Using the chenille needle, work the bow following the step-by-step instructions.

Corner sprays

Using the photograph as a guide for colour placement, embroider the four corner sprays in a similar manner to those in the wreath, omitting the bullion roses.

Outer bouquets

Embroider the four outer bouquets in a similar manner to the bouquets in the wreath.

Construction

See page 131.

B O U Q U E T

C O R N E R S P R A Y

MILDLY AND SOFT THE WESTERN BREEZE
JUST KISSED THE LAKE, JUST STIRR'D THE TREES,
AND THE PLEASED LAKE, LIKE MAIDEN COY,
TREMBLED BUT DIMPLED NOT FOR JOY.

CANTO III, STANZA 2, THE LADY OF THE LAKE
WALTER SCOTT

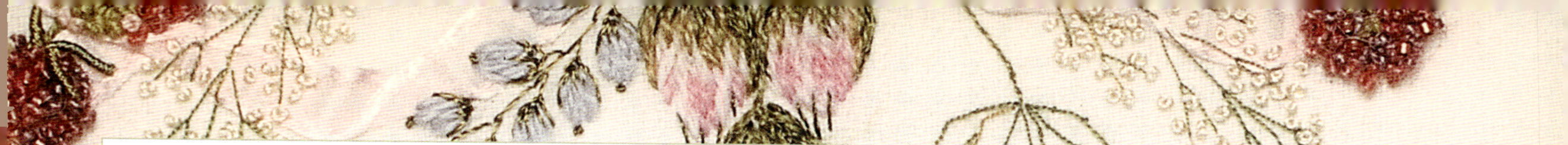

Threads, Ribbons, Beads and Needles

Paterna Persian yarn

A = 326 vy lt plum (2 skeins)

B = 327 ultra vy lt plum (2 skeins)

C = 490 dk flesh

D = 494 vy lt flesh

E = 654 lt olive green

F = 906 ultra lt American beauty (3 skeins)

G = D392 lt dolphin

H = D531 verdigris

Kirra hand dyed yarns 2 ply wool

I = 114 khaki green (3 skeins)

J = 116 hazelnut brown (3 skeins)

K = 207 dk khaki green (3 skeins)

Littlewood Fleece yarns 2ply wool

L = 13 pink rainbow

M = 30 red rainbow

Anchor Marlitt stranded rayon

N = 826 olive green

O = 827 dk olive green

P = 1036 lt champagne (2 skeins)

Q = 1207 shell pink

Anchor stranded cotton

R = 271 ultra lt dusky pink

S = 280 olive

T = 842 vy lt khaki green

U = 845 dk khaki green

Colour Streams 'Silken Strands' stranded silk

V = 26 Tuscan olive

W = 36 salt bush

Colour Streams 'Ophir' silk

X = 26 Tuscan olive (2 skeins)

Maria George Delica beads

Y = DBR 106 transparent pink lustre (3 pkts)

Mokuba no. 4546 Crepe Georgette 9mm (3/8") wide satin edge ribbon

Z = 3m (3yds 12") no. 31 pink

Kacoonda hand dyed 4mm (3/16") wide silk ribbon

AA = 3m (3yds 12") no. 3F wedgewood blue

Needles

No. 1 milliner's needle

No. 3 milliner's needle

No. 9 milliner's needle

No. 9 crewel needle

No. 18 chenille needle

No. 22 chenille needle

Embroidery Key

All embroidery is worked with one strand unless otherwise specified.

Pink bow = Z and R (appliqué)

Wild roses

Petals = A, B and F (long and short stitch)

Petal highlights = Q (straight stitch)

Centre = S, T and U (2 strands, French knot, 1 wrap)

Leaves = J and K (long and short stitch)

Leaf veins = O (stem stitch, straight stitch)

Leaf outline = O (straight stitch)

Calyx = K (fly stitch, straight stitch)

Stem = K (stem stitch)

Wild rosebuds

Petals = A, B and F (long and short stitch)

Calyx = J and K (long and short stitch)

Calyx outline = O (straight stitch)

Tips = O (straight stitch, fly stitch)

Stems = J (grab stitch, stem stitch)

Leaves = I and J (straight stitch)

Leaf veins and outline = N (stem stitch, straight stitch)

Berries

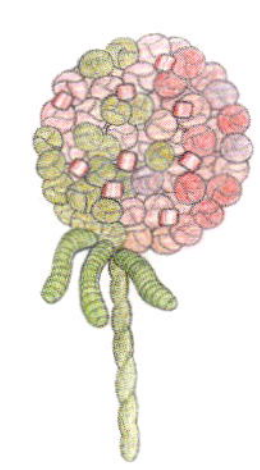

Berries = E, H and M or E, H and L or H, L and M (French knot, 2 wraps)

Berry highlights = R and Y (2 strands, 4 - 9 beads)

Sepals = X (3 bullion knots, 15 - 17 wraps)

Stems = I or J (stem stitch)

Leaves = I and X (straight stitch)

Bullion roses

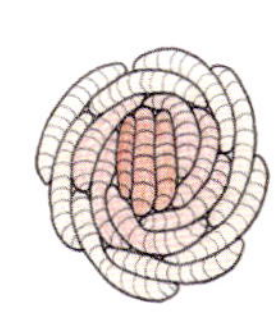

Centre = C (3 bullion knots, 8 wraps)

Inner petals = D (5 or 6 bullion knots, 10 - 14 wraps)

Outer petals = B (6 to 8 bullion knots, 12 - 16 wraps)

Leaves = I and W (fly stitch)

~ EMBROIDERY KEY ~

Bullion rosebuds

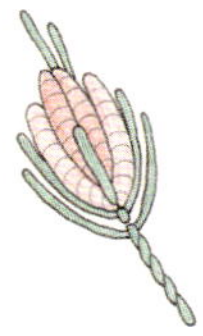

Inner petals = C (2 bullion knots, 8 wraps)

Outer petals = D (2 bullion knots, 9 wraps) or none

Calyx = I (fly stitch, straight stitch)

Leaves = I and W (fly stitch)

Stems = I and W (back stitch, stem stitch)

Tips = I or W (straight stitch) or none

French knot Gypsophila

Stems = V (fly stitch, straight stitch)

Flowers in spray = P (2 strands, French knot, 1 wrap)

Beaded Gypsophilia

Stems = V (fly stitch, straight stitch)

Flowers = Y and R (2 strands, beading)

Blue bow = AA (ribbon loop, straight stitch, twisted ribbon stitch)

Queen Anne's lace

Stems = V (stem stitch)

Bracts = V (straight stitch, couching)

Petals = P (2 strands, French knot, 1 wrap)

Centre = Y and R (2 strands, beading)

Blue sprays

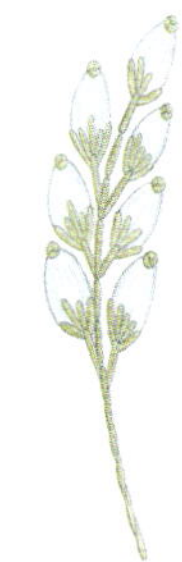

Stems = N (back stitch, stem stitch)

Bud = G (straight stitch)

Tips = N (French knot, 1 wrap)

Calyx = N (fly stitch, straight stitch)

~ STEP-BY-STEP ~

BERRY

The plump berries are arranged in groups of three or four using tightly packed French knots. They vary in colour from shades of green and pale pink through to the darker shades of pink. Three bullion knots form the sepals at the base of each. Our instructions show working a ripe berry.

1. Draw the circle for the berry shape. Using the darkest shade of green, work a few French knots.

2. Change to the medium pink and work French knots, placing some among the green knots.

3. Change to darker pink. Tightly fill berry with French knots, mixing them with previous colours.

4. Add several small beads, stitching them randomly over the French knots.

5. Berry sepals. Work three bullion knots at the base of the berry, anchoring them so they are slightly curved.

BLUE SPRAY

The creative combination of simple stitches and varying thread textures forms this appealing spray.

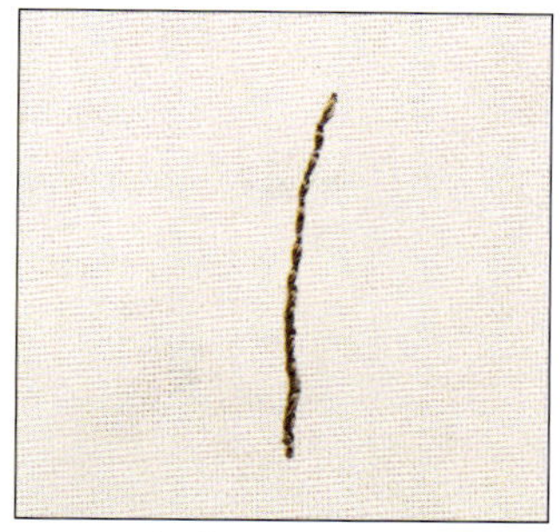

1. Stitch the main stem with back stitch and stem stitch.

2. Beginning at the centre and working out to the sides, work the first blue bud in straight stitch.

3. Continue in the same manner for the remaining buds.

4. Work a few tiny straight stitches over the base of each bud. Work a French knot at the tip.

5. Embroider a fly stitch around the base with a long anchoring stitch to connect it to the main stem.

BLUE RIBBON BOW

The bow is formed by stitching through the fabric rather than being tied and then stitched on the surface.

Work the bows over the rose and gypsophila stems in the bouquets.

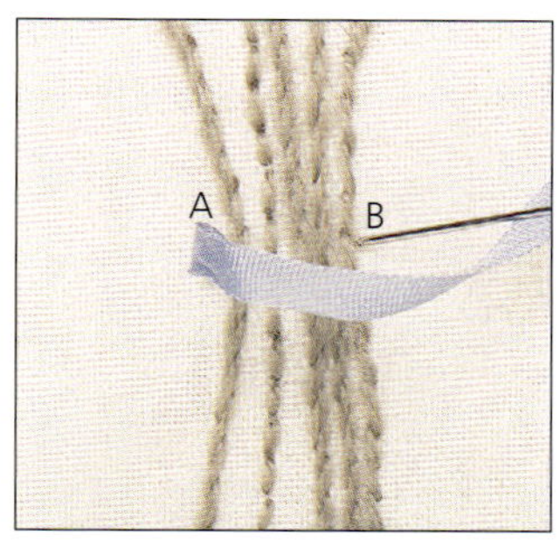

1. Loops. Bring the ribbon to the front at A. Take to the back at B.

2. Pull the ribbon through. Bring the ribbon to the front at C. Take to the back next to C.

3. Pull the ribbon through forming a soft rounded loop 2cm (3/4") long.

4. Work a second loop at C.

5. Knot. Work two vertical straight stitches over C to form the knot.

6. Tails. Work two twisted ribbon stitches. Secure each with a tiny straight stitch if necessary.

The well loved Australian icon,

the Laughing Kookaburra is instantly recognisable in the lifelike threadpainting. The red flowering gum and the golden wattle add wonderful touches of colour and texture on the ivory wool.

Requirements

Fabric

107cm x 75cm wide (42" x 30") piece of ivory wool blanketing

123cm x 91cm wide (49" x 36") piece of green cotton print

Supplies

10cm (4") square of white felt

107cm x 75cm wide (42" x 30") piece of thin wadding

3.2m (3yd 18") grey-green mini piping

36cm (14") quilting hoop

White tissue paper

Sharp HB pencil

Threads & Needles

See page 78.

This Design Uses

Fly stitch, French knot
Ghiordes knot
Interlocked straight stitch
Satin stitch, Split stitch
Straight stitch

• • •

Preparation for Embroidery

See the pattern sheet for the embroidery design.

Preparing the fabric

Fold the fabric in half across the width. Using pale machine sewing thread, stitch a row of tacking along the fold line. Refold the blanket along its length. Tack along the fold line in the same manner.

Transferring the design

Trace the design, including the placement marks, onto the tissue paper. Position the tracing on the right side of the blanketing, aligning the placement marks with the lines of tacking. Pin the tracing in place.

Using pale machine sewing thread and small tacking stitches, tack through the tissue paper and the blanketing along the design lines.

Most tacking threads marking the design can remain in the work permanently as the embroidery will cover them.

Lightly moisten the tissue paper with a damp sponge, wait a few seconds, then carefully remove the paper.

THE FINISHED BLANKET MEASURES 107CM X 75CM WIDE (42" X 30")

EMBROIDERY

See the step-by-step instructions on pages 80 and 81 for working interlocked straight stitch, the wing, the wattle and the gum blossom.

See the pattern sheet for the stitch direction diagram and the templates for the gum blossom and the gumnut.

Use the crewel needle for the stranded threads and the chenille needle for the remaining threads. Place the fabric in the hoop for all embroidery, except when working the fly stitches and the Ghiordes knots. Follow the stitch direction diagram for stitch placement and refer to the photograph for colour changes throughout the design.

"When beginning an area, choose a length of yarn from the middle of the colour range and work scattered straight stitches to indicate the stitch direction."

JENNY

Order of work

Kookaburra

Eye

Fill the eye with satin stitches using the black thread and add the white highlight. Outline the lower edge of the eye with pale blue and stitch two straight stitches at the corner of the eye. Add the black outlines above and below the eye *(diag 1)*.

Diag 1

Beak

Embroider the upper beak in the blue threads and add the outline along the lower edge in the brown thread.

Work the lower beak in the flesh and brown shades.

Mask and head

Work the marking over the eye in black. With the darkest brown, work the mask around the eye and forehead. Radiating the stitching out from the mask, fill the remainder of the head. Allow the stitches to be feathery at the edges.

Wing

Referring to the photograph as a guide for colour placement and following the step-by-step instructions, embroider the wing.

Chest and body

Scatter fly stitches for the feather markings in the same manner as the wing. Fill each 'V' with straight stitch.

Using interlocked straight stitch, fill in the remainder of the chest and body, allowing the stitches at the edges to be feathery.

Complete the lower edge of the bird with feathery stitches after the branch and claws have been embroidered.

Tail

Embroider the markings with straight stitches, giving a slightly banded appearance. Fill in the top and the end with interlocked straight stitch.

Claw

Stitch the claw with interlocked straight stitch after the branch has been worked. Add the details with straight stitch.

Wattle

Branch and foliage

Work the branch with interlocked straight stitch, adding extra stitches on the smaller ends for twigs. Stitch the markings on the branch with the dark denim thread. Embroider the stems and leaves for the blossom using the two shades of green.

Flowers

Work the blossom with Ghiordes knots, referring to the step-by-step instructions.

Red flowering gum

Stems and leaves

Working from the vein outwards and angling the stitches, embroider the leaves with satin stitch. Work the stem and vein for each leaf in split stitch, noting the colour changes on the stem.

Blossom

Work the lower blossom following the step-by-step instructions. Stitch the upper blossom in a similar manner, adding the pistil before stitching the stamens.

Gumnut

Cut the padding from the felt using the template on the pattern sheet. Position the felt piece and attach with blanket stitch around the outer edge.

Work a row of satin stitch along the rim of the gumnut. Fill the inner and the outer surfaces with interlocked straight stitch. Add the stalk in split stitch. Work the outline with the black and mahogany threads. Embroider the pistil with split stitch, adding a French knot to the end.

CONSTRUCTION

See page 131.

Threads *and* Needles

DMC stranded cotton

A = 300 vy dk mahogany

B = 304 lt garnet

C = 309 deep rose

D = 310 black

E = 733 med olive green

F = 754 lt peach

G = 781 vy dk topaz

H = 973 bright canary

I = 3705 dk melon

J = 3776 lt mahogany

DMC Broder Médicis wool

K = 8418 med moss green

L = 8419 moss green

Gumnut Yarns 'Buds' perlé silk

M = 945 med hazelnut

N = 966 med dk chocolate dip

O = 967 dk chocolate dip

P = 969 ultra dk chocolate dip

Q = 999 nearly black

Gumnut Yarns 'Daisies' fine wool

R = 708 very dk lemon crush

Gumnut Yarns 'Stars' stranded silk

S = 344 lt denim

T = 346 med dk denim

U = 348 vy dk denim

V = 349 ultra dk denim

W = 405 med sky blue

X = 825 med peach melba

Y = 855 med salmon pink

Z = 863 lt flesh

AA = 865 med flesh

AB = 867 dk flesh

AC = 869 ultra dk flesh

AD = 949 ultra dk hazelnut

AE = 969 ultra dk chocolate dip

AF = 990 white

AG = 991 ecru

AH = 998 very dk pewter

Gumnut Yarns 'Tulips' mohair

AI = 383 lt cornflower

AJ = 386 med dk cornflower

AK = 867 dk flesh

AL = 869 ultra dk flesh

AM = 943 lt hazelnut

AN = 945 med hazelnut

AO = 947 dk hazelnut

AP = 949 ultra dk hazelnut

AQ = 969 ultra dk chocolate dip

AR = 990 white

AS = 991 ecru

AT = 992 vy lt pewter

AU = 999 nearly black

Needles

No. 7 crewel needle

No. 22 chenille needle

Take care with tension, keeping the stitches relaxed and even.

Don't overcrowd the area with too many stitches. Aim to cover the fabric, not smother it.

Depending on the texture required, for example, the kookaburra's beak, the previous stitches are not split and therefore give a smooth finish.

For a textured appearance, for example feathers, the previous stitches can be split or overlap each other.

~ Embroidery Key ~

All embroidery is worked with one strand unless otherwise specified.

Kookaburra

Eye

Pupil = D (satin stitch)

Highlight = AR (straight stitch)

Lower outline = D and T (straight stitch)

Corner marking = T (straight stitch)

Upper outline = O (straight stitch)

Beak

Upper beak = T, U, V, W and AH (interlocked straight stitch), AR (straight stitch)

Upper beak outline = A and AH (straight stitch)

Lower beak = Y, Z, AA, AB, AC, AF and AG (interlocked straight stitch)

Mask and head

Marking over eye = Q (straight stitch)

Mask = AK, AL, AN, AO, AP and AS (interlocked straight stitch)

Head = AM, AN, AO, AR and AT (interlocked straight stitch)

Wing

Feather markings = AI, AO and AQ (fly stitch), AI, AJ, AM, AN, AO and AQ (straight stitch)

Wing filling = AN, AO and AQ (interlocked straight stitch)

Wing outline = AU (split stitch, straight stitch)

Chest and body

Feather markings = AM and AN (fly stitch), AM, AN, AR and AS (straight stitch)

Chest and body filling = AM, AN, AR and AS (interlocked straight stitch)

Shading on neck = AO (straight stitch)

Tail

Feather markings = AM, AN, AO and AQ (straight stitch)

Tail filling = AM, AN, AO, AR and AS (interlocked straight stitch, straight stitch)

Claw = M (interlocked straight stitch)

Claw markings = Q (straight stitch)

Wattle

Branch = N, O and P (interlocked straight stitch)

Marking = V (4 strands, straight stitch)

Leaves = K and L (interlocked straight stitch)

Stems = K and L (split stitch, straight stitch)

Blossom = R (Ghiordes knot)

Red flowering gum

Leaves = K and L (satin stitch)

Stems and veins = G, R and AK (split stitch, straight stitch)

Blossoms

Outer surface = E, F, G, H and I (interlocked straight stitch)

Pistil = C (split stitch), H (French knot, 1 wrap)

Stamens = B, C and I (straight stitch), H (French knot, 1 wrap)

Stems = E, G and I (split stitch, straight stitch)

Outline = A and D (split stitch)

Gumnut

Rim = J (satin stitch)

Inner surface = A, F and G (interlocked straight stitch)

Outer surface = E, F, G, H and I (interlocked straight stitch)

Outline = A and D (split stitch)

Pistil = I (split stitch) and H (2 strands, French knot, 1 wrap)

Interlocked straight stitch

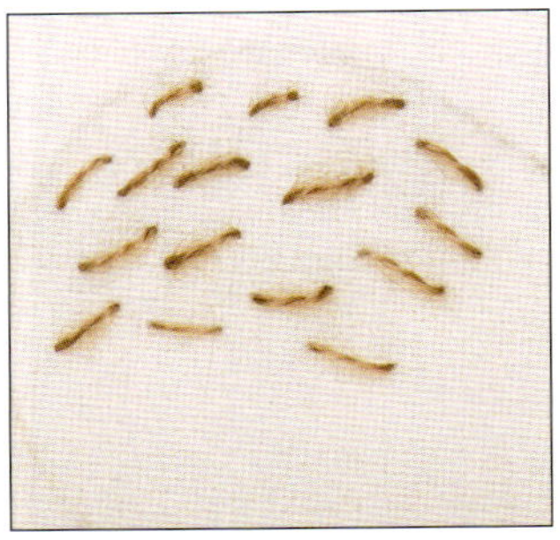

1. With one of the main colours in the design, work a few straight stitches to indicate the stitch direction.

2. Keeping the tension even and not too firm, begin to fill the area with straight stitches of varying lengths.

3. Continue filling the shape. Overlap the stitches when changing direction.

4. Change colour as necessary and complete filling the design area.

Wattle

The wattle blossom is created with Ghiordes knots stitched to form a circular shape. We have used a stranded thread for photographic purposes.

1. Take the thread to the back at A. Leave a tail on the front. Emerge at B.

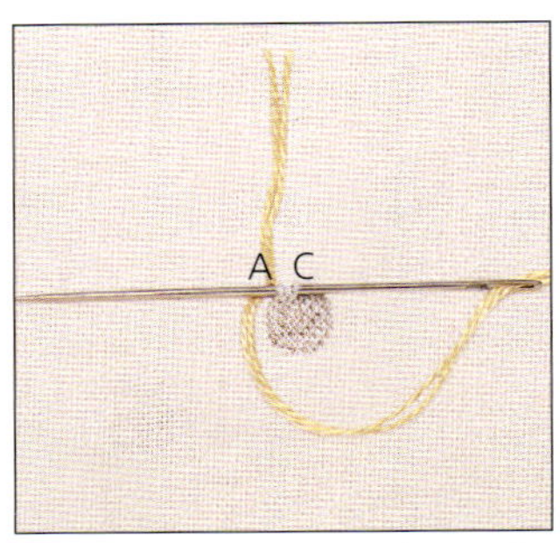

2. Pull the thread through. Take to the back at C and emerge at A.

3. Pull the thread to tighten the stitch.

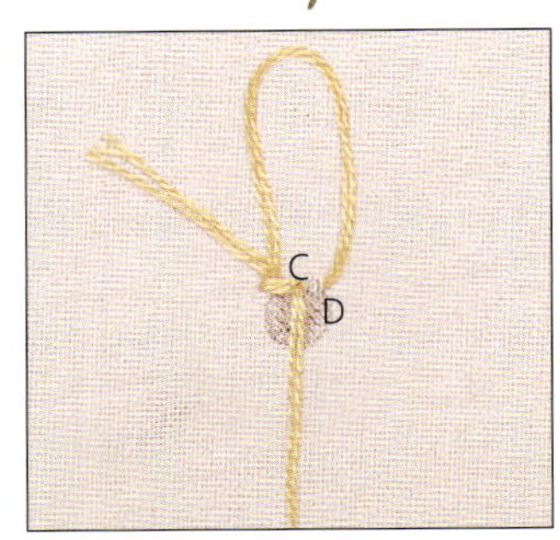

4. Take the thread to the back at D and emerge at C, leaving a loop.

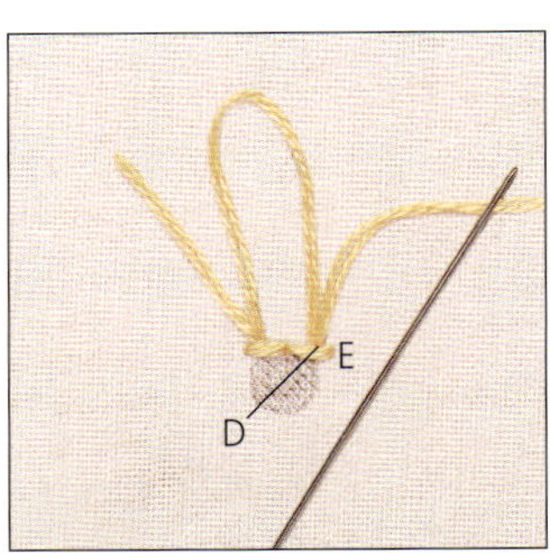

5. Take thread to the back at E and emerge at D to form the next stitch.

6. Work a few more knots forming a circular shape.

7. Cut the loops and trim to a suitable length. Fluff out the ends a little.

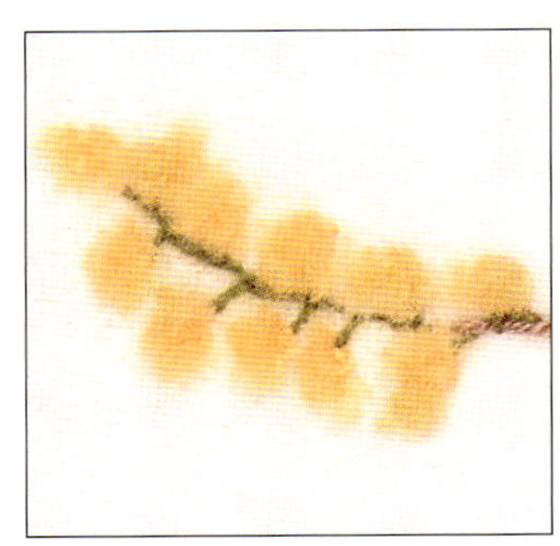

8. Repeat for each blossom, then work the stems with straight stitch.

Stitching the Kookaburra's Wing

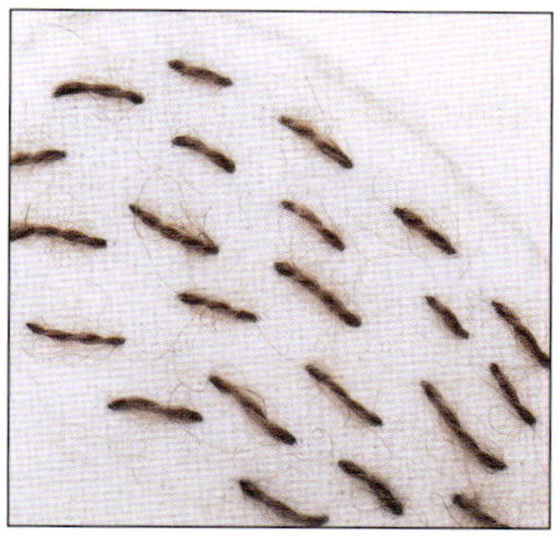

1. With one of the main colours for the wing, work some straight stitches to indicate the stitch direction.

2. Place random fly stitches and straight stitches following the stitch direction. Vary the size and colour.

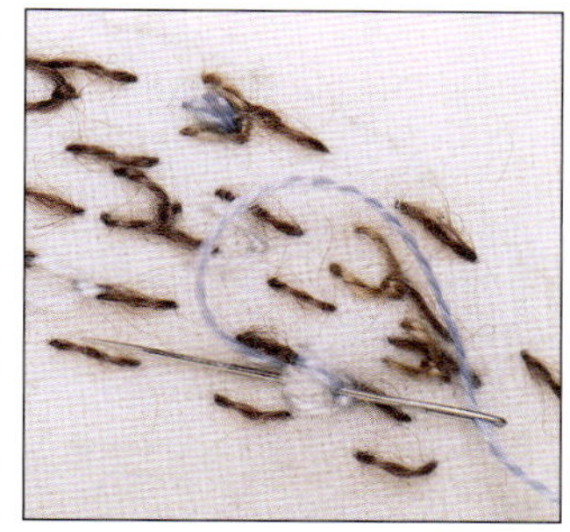

3. Fill each fly stitch with straight stitches.

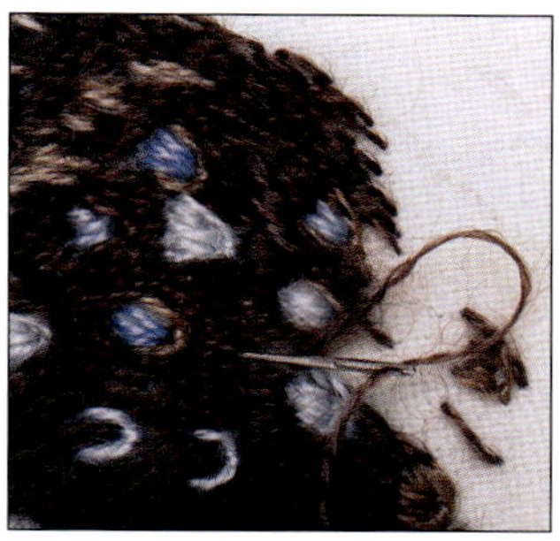

4. Fill in the remainder of the wing with interlocked straight stitch until the area is closely covered.

5. Work a partial outline along the front of the wing in straight stitch and split stitch.

Gum Blossom

Our instructions demonstrate stitching the lower blossom in the design.

1. Using the template on the pattern sheet, cut the padding from the felt.

2. Position the felt piece and attach with blanket stitch around the edge.

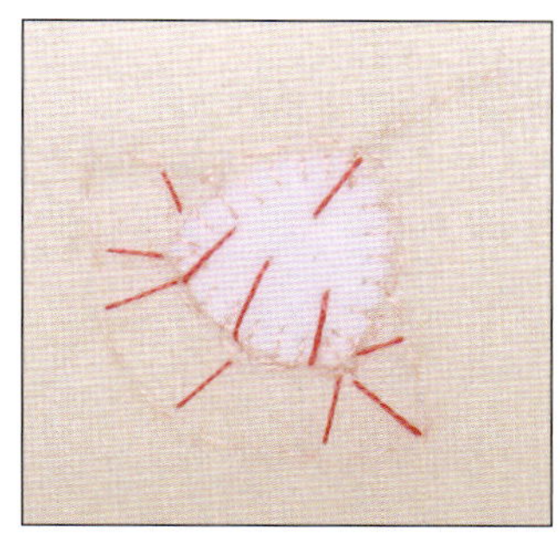

3. Work a few straight stitches to indicate stitch direction. Repeat for the stamens.

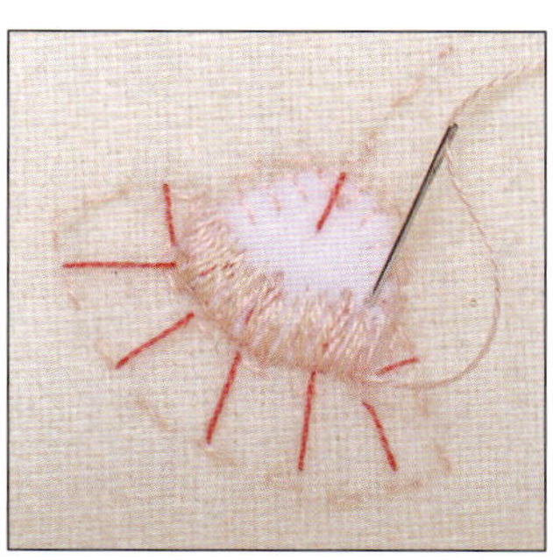

4. Begin to fill the outer surface with interlocked straight stitch, changing colour as necessary.

5. When the area is filled, embroider stamens, adding highlights.

6. Work the stem in split stitch. Add French knots at the ends of some of the stamens.

7. Stitch the outline along the base of the gumnut in split stitch.

Glorious blue-violet ribbons trail softly across the ends of this beautiful floral design, stitched onto rich cream wool flannel. Sprinkled with dainty posies of roses, daisies and forget-me-nots, this superb blanket would be equally suited for use in a nursery or as an elegant throw.

Requirements

Fabric

120cm x 80cm wide (47" x 32") piece of ivory doctor's flannel

132cm x 92cm wide (52" x 37") piece of ivory winter twill

Supplies

3.7m (4yd) dusty baby pink mini piping

120cm x 80cm wide (47" x 32") piece of thin wadding

Tracing paper

Water-soluble fabric marker

Fine black permanent pen

15cm (6") embroidery hoop

Threads & Needles

See page 88.

Preparation for Embroidery

See page 131 for preparing the fabric and the design placement diagram and the pattern sheet for the embroidery designs.

This Design Uses

Bullion knot, Bullion loop
Detached chain
Detached herringbone stitch
Fly stitch, French knot
Granitos, Stem stitch
Straight stitch

Transferring the design

Using the pen, trace the embroidery designs, including any placement marks, onto tracing paper.

Bows, ribbons and flowers

Tape the corner bow design tracing to a window or light box. Place one corner of the doctor's flannel over the tracing, matching the placement marks on the design with the tacked lines. Tape in place. With the fabric marker, trace the design onto the fabric. Repeat for the remaining corners.

Tape the tracing of the ribbon design to the window or light box. Place the upper edge of the doctor's flannel over the tracing, matching the placement marks on the design with the tacking. Tape in place and trace the design with the fabric marker. Repeat on the lower edge.

Posies and sprays

Follow the design placement diagram on the pattern sheet for the position and orientation of the floral posies and sprays.

Place the traced posy in the required position and pin. Using the tapestry needle, pierce the tracing paper at the end of the longest stem and at the centre of each of the three roses and daisies. Using the fabric marker, mark a dot through each hole. Repeat for the remaining posies.

Mark the position of the bud sprays in a similar manner.

by Julie Graue

The finished blanket measures 120cm x 80cm wide (47" x 32")

Embroidery

See the step-by-step instructions on page 89 for the bullion knot rose and the shadow work bow.

Use the milliner's needle for working the bullion knots and loops, the tapestry needle for the bows and ribbons and the crewel needle for all other embroidery.

Order of work

Floral posy

Embroider the three roses first. At the base of the uppermost rose, work three or four French knots. Add four straight stitches for the rose stems. Work two or three straight stitches across the stems to hold them together *(diag 1)*.

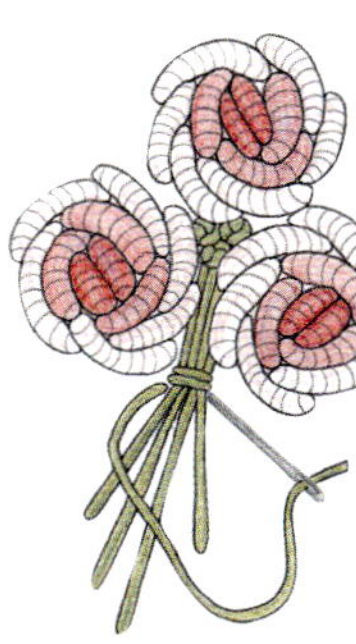

Diag 1

Work the bud with one bullion knot for the centre and two for the petals, one of which has a long anchoring stitch at the tip.

At the base of the bud, embroider a fly stitch with a long anchoring stitch, then add a French knot between the bud and the fly stitch. At the tip, work two straight stitches.

Using the photograph as a guide for placement, embroider three pairs of fly stitch leaves. Give the leaves a curved appearance by making one arm of the fly stitch longer than the other.

Work each daisy with four bullion loop petals. Using a new thread, work a detached chain stitch to secure the end of each loop. Add a pink French knot for the centre.

Scatter six French knot forget-me-nots around the design.

Stitch a cluster of three pink French knots between each pair of leaves and embroider single French knots among the flowers.

Bud spray

Embroider the larger bud with two bullion knots for the centre, with the second knot slightly longer than the first. Stitch two curved bullion knots for the petals, working one with a long anchoring stitch.

Embroider the smaller bud in the same manner, with only one bullion knot for the centre. Add two straight stitches to the tip of each bud, and a fly stitch around the base. Work a straight stitch along half the length of the centre petals of the larger bud and then the stems in stem stitch. Embroider the fly stitch leaves.

Bows, ribbons and flowers

Stitch the shadow work bows and ribbons referring to the step-by-step instructions.

Embroider the flowers and leaves in a similar manner as before, referring to the step-by-step instructions for the side view rose on the ribbon design. For the bow design, work the fly stitch around the bud with a long anchoring stitch, adding detached chain leaves and a French knot.

Scatter French knots among the flowers on the ribbons and add the granitos spots.

Construction

See page 131.

- Threads *and* Needles -

Madeira stranded silk

A = 0502 baby pink

B = 0815 ultra lt shell pink (2 pkts)

C = 0901 lt blue-violet (4 pkts)

D = 2014 ultra lt tan

E = 2401 soft white (2 pkts)

Madeira stranded cotton

F = 0912 dk cobalt blue (2 pkts)

DMC no. 5 perlé cotton

G = 3013 lt khaki green (2 skeins)

Paterna Persian yarn

H = 923 lt wood rose

I = 947 lt cranberry (2 skeins)

J = 948 ultra lt cranberry (2 skeins)

Needles

No. 3 milliner's needle

No. 8 crewel needle

No. 26 tapestry needle

- Embroidery Key -

All embroidery is worked with one strand unless otherwise specified.

Floral posy

Roses

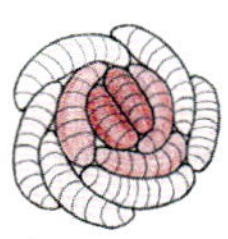

Centre = H (2 bullion knots, 6 wraps)

Inner petals = I (3 bullion knots, 8 wraps)

Outer petals = J (6 bullion knots, 10 wraps)

French knots = G (French knot, 1 wrap)

Stems = G (straight stitch)

Bud

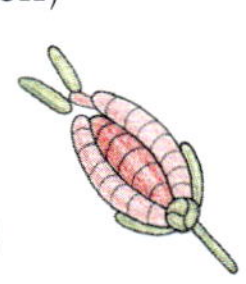

Centre = H (bullion knot, 6 wraps)

Petals = I (2 bullion knots, 8 wraps)

Calyx = G (fly stitch, French knot, 1 wrap)

Bud tip = G (straight stitch)

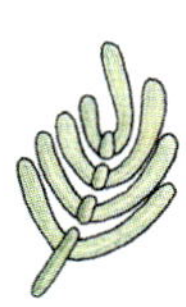

Leaves = G (fly stitch)

Daisies

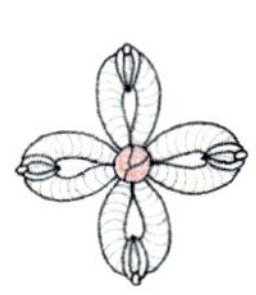

Petals = E (2 strands, 4 bullion loops, 20 wraps, 1 strand, detached chain)

Centre = A (2 strands, French knot, 2 wraps)

Forget-me-nots

Petals = C (2 strands, French knot, 2 wraps)

Centre = D (2 strands, French knot, 2 wraps)

Dots = B (2 strands, French knot, 2 wraps)

Bud spray

Buds

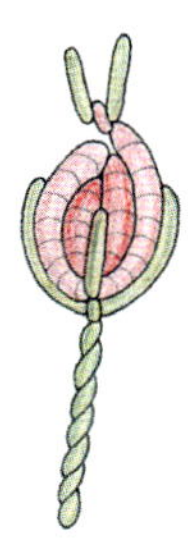

Centre = H (1 or 2 bullion knots, 6 wraps)

Petals = I (2 bullion knots, 8 - 10 wraps)

Calyx = G (fly stitch)

Bud tip = G (straight stitch)

Stems and leaves = G (stem stitch, fly stitch)

Bows, ribbons and flowers

Bow and ribbon = C (2 strands, back stitch), F (4 strands, detached herringbone stitch)

Rose

Centre = H (2 bullion knots, 6 wraps)

Inner petals = I (3 bullion knots, 8 wraps)

Outer petals = J (5 or 6 bullion knots, 10 wraps)

Leaves = G (fly stitch)

Buds

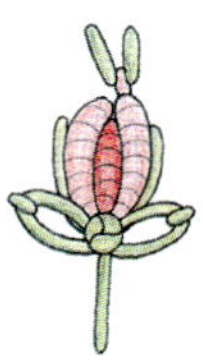

Centre = H (bullion knot, 6 wraps)

Petals = I (2 bullion knots, 8 wraps)

Foliage = G (fly stitch, French knot, 1 wrap, detached chain, straight stitch)

Daisies

Petals = E (2 strands, 3 bullion loops, 20 wraps, 1 strand, detached chain stitch)

Centre = A (2 strands, French knot, 2 wraps)

Forget-me-nots

Petals = C (2 strands, French knot, 2 wraps)

Centre = D (2 strands, French knot, 2 wraps)

Dots = E (4 strands, granitos), B (2 strands, French knot, 2 wraps)

Bullion Knot Rose

Refer to the stitch glossary on page 124 for instructions on stitching a bullion knot. By altering the placement of the inner and outer rows of bullion knots in relation to the centre, you can create a different orientation, for example a side view rose. This is illustrated in step 6.

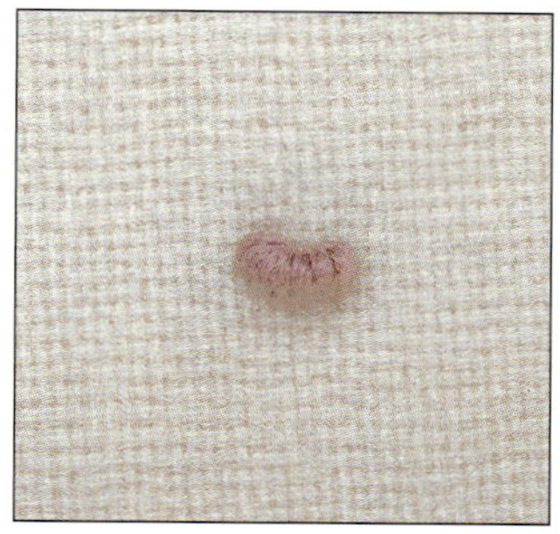

1. Centre. Using the darkest pink thread, work a 4mm (3/16") long bullion knot with 6 wraps.

2. Work a second bullion knot close to and parallel to the first.

3. Inner petals. Change to the medium shade of pink. Work an 8 wrap bullion knot, curving it slightly.

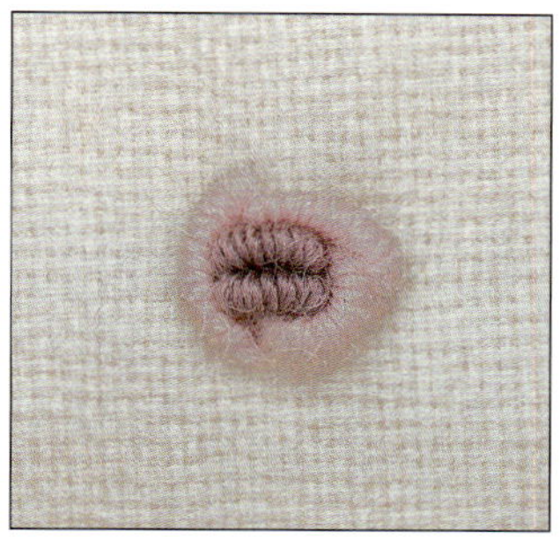

4. Work two more 8 wrap bullion knots surrounding the centre. Overlap their ends slightly.

5. Outer petals. Change to lightest shade. Work six 10 wrap bullion knots around rose. Overlap ends slightly.

6. Side view rose. Work the centre and inner petals as before. Position the outer petals towards the base.

Shadow Work Bow

This variation of shadow work is stitched in two stages. So that the colour shows through the doctor's flannel, a lighter shade is used on the front and a darker shade with extra strands is used on the back. Place the fabric in the embroidery hoop and use the tapestry needle when working the detached herringbone stitch.

The photographs illustrate stitching a bow loop. Work the ribbon ties in a similar manner.

1. Outline. Work the outline around the shape with small, regular back stitches on the right side of the fabric.

2. Detached herringbone. Secure a new thread on the wrong side at A. Slide the needle under both rows of back stitch at B and C.

3. Pull the thread through. Slide the needle under the stitches at D and E.

4. Continue working the detached herringbone stitches to fill the shape.

5. Stitch into the new shape, ensuring that the thread does not trail over the background fabric at the crossover.

6. Complete the second part of the shape. To secure, weave the thread through the previous stitches.

Carolyn has used some of her most beautiful embroidered flowers and foliage on this blanket. She has then incorporated some particularly whimsical ideas.

Mother Rabbit is beautifully embroidered in soft wools and completely dressed, right down to her lace trimmed bloomers and suede shoes. She carries a woven basket of ribbon flowers.

Raised embroidery provides a life-like appearance for the surrounding scene.

Requirements

Fabric

120cm x 90cm wide (47" x 36") piece of ivory wool blanketing

132cm x 102cm wide (52" x 41") piece of floral cotton print

20cm (8") square of 25 count *Lugana*

15cm x 50cm wide (6" x 20") piece of cream homespun

20cm x 40cm wide (8" x 16") piece of blue chambray

20cm x 25cm wide (8" x 10") piece of white organdy

12cm x 14cm wide (5" x 6") piece of white batiste

50cm x 60cm wide (20" x 24") piece of white nylon tulle

3cm x 8cm wide (1" x 3") piece of burgundy ultra suede

Supplies

3.9m (4yd 10") cream satin piping

25cm (10") square of grey felt

8cm (3") square of white felt

25cm (10") square of appliqué paper

Small amount of lightweight non woven interfacing

60cm x 3mm wide (24" x 1/8") white satin ribbon

10cm x 5mm wide (4" x 3/16") white lace edging

18cm x 15mm wide (7" x 5/8") white lace edging

Cream machine sewing thread

Burgundy machine sewing thread to match the burgundy suede

Grey *Nymo* thread

Small amount of polyester fibre-fill

5cm (2") length of pipe cleaner

10cm (4") embroidery hoop

36cm (14") quilting hoop

Water-soluble fabric marker

Fine black permanent pen

Threads, Ribbons, Beads & Needles

See page 103.

Preparation for Embroidery

See the pattern sheet for the embroidery designs, felt templates, rabbit patterns and for working the needlepoint.

Preparing the blanketing

Fold the blanketing in half across the width. While folded, using pale machine sewing thread, stitch a row of tacking along the fold line. Refold the blanketing along its length. Tack along the fold line in the same manner.

Transferring the design

Trace the embroidery design, including the placement marks, onto the tulle with the black pen. Let the ink dry thoroughly. Pin the tulle in position on the blanketing, aligning the placement marks with the tacking. Trace the design with the water-soluble fabric marker. Remove the tulle and tack along the design lines with the cream machine sewing thread. Most of the tacking threads marking the design can remain in the work permanently as the embroidery will cover them. Remove all visible marks left by the fabric marker with a damp cloth.

Preparing the rabbit and felt pieces

Cut out the rabbit body from the cream homespun. Cut along the marked line for the legs and clip into the corners. Turn under the seam allowances on all edges and tack the body into position.

Trace the templates onto the smooth side of the appliqué paper. Fuse to the felt pieces and cut out all the shapes. Peel off the backing paper. Refer to the step-by-step instructions for working the rabbit head and the blackberry.

Embroidery

See pages 106 and 107 for the step-by-step instructions for working the rabbit head and the blackberry. Refer to the pattern sheet for the stitch direction diagram and for the charts for the beehive and the basket.

Order of work

Rabbit

Head

After tacking the body in place, work the head and ears following the step-by-step instructions.

Feet

Tuck the felt feet shapes under the legs and hand stitch in place.

Cover the ankle area with long and short stitch. Cut out the shoes from the burgundy suede and place onto the feet, slightly overlapping the long and short stitches. Using the burgundy sewing thread, hand stitch into position around the edges.

Paw

Hand stitch the two pieces together around the curved edge, leaving the base open below the marked line. Fill the paw with fibre-fill. Hand stitch the opening closed. Work long and short stitch on both sides of the paw above the marked line. Angle the stitches towards the tip of the paw.

Completing the rabbit

Following the instructions on pages 131-133, complete the rabbit and her clothing when all the surrounding embroidery has been worked. Add the basket of flowers last.

..... *Using Appliqué Paper* .....

Appliqué paper is most commonly used to bond or fuse two layers of fabric together as part of the technique of appliqué. It can, however, be useful for other purposes.

In stumpwork or raised embroidery, the design can easily be transferred onto padding by tracing the design onto the smooth side of the appliqué paper and then fusing it to the underside of the padding. The shape is then cut out and applied to the design, either by fusing the layers or hand stitching the shape in place.

Using appliqué paper gives the fabric the benefit of added stiffness, thereby firming up the surface on which to embroider.

Fabrics used for padding, such as felt, are given a smooth surface on which to embroider when the glue side is placed uppermost.

Wild roses

Flowers

Embroider five petals for each flower, leaving a space for the colonial knots at the centre. Work each petal with a granitos of five stitches laid side by side. Add three more stitches over the top to give a smooth and plump appearance. Run the needle under the stitches to help position them.

Using the darker pink, work two or three straight stitches and a fly stitch to form the tip highlights of each petal. Changing to green, work a short straight stitch between each petal, from the base to where the petals begin to separate. Embroider the petal inner highlights by adding three straight stitches of different lengths radiating from the base. Add the colonial knot centre.

Small rosebuds

Begin by working a granitos of three stitches. Add a slightly longer stitch over the top. Using the darker pink, work a straight stitch and a fly stitch to form the tip highlights. At the bud tip, add a fly stitch and a straight stitch, then work the straight stitch calyx at the base of the bud.

Large rosebuds

Begin with a granitos of seven stitches. Add a slightly longer stitch over the top to achieve a pointed appearance. Embroider the second petal with three stitches across the lower section of the bud, using the same two holes and keeping the stitches to the right *(diag 1)*. Embroider the third petal in the same manner, working in the opposite direction.

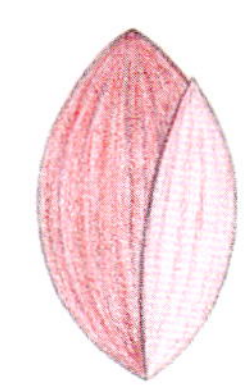

Diag 1

Work the calyx in the same manner as the small rosebuds. At the tip of the bud, embroider two tiny fly stitches with long anchoring stitches.

Rosehips

Use the six sets of three oval shapes as padding for the rosehips. For each hip stitch the smallest piece of felt, glue side down, to the blanketing. Stitch the medium piece over it in the same manner and then the largest piece.

Starting at the stem end of the rosehip, cover the felt with long and short stitch, angling the stitches towards the two ends. Embroider a highlight on each rosehip. Add several straight stitches in the metallic thread.

At the tip, complete the rosehip with pistil stitches of different lengths, radiating from a central point.

Stems

For some stems, lay and couch the green wool, then whip with silk thread. Embroider the remaining stems in whipped reverse chain stitch.

Leaves

Embroider the fly stitch leaves randomly throughout the design. All are worked in the same manner, although the size may vary. Start at the tip of the leaf and work towards the base. Make an uneven fly stitch at the tip and work the next stitches so that the shape of the leaf fills out in the middle and then comes in again at the base. Finish with a smocker's knot.

Blackberries

Work the berry and sepals following the step-by-step instructions. There are three combinations of threads and beads for the berries.

Stems and leaves

Embroider the stems in whipped reverse chain stitch. Add fly stitch thorns to some of the stems, anchoring them to the stem. Work the leaves with fly stitch, adding a smocker's knot at the base. Finish the knot with a long anchoring stitch to attach the leaf to the stem.

Spent flowers

Work the stamens with nine or ten straight stitches. Add French and colonial knots at the ends.

Embroider the sepals with fly stitches, angling them away from the flower.

Work the stems in the same manner as the blackberry stems, omitting the thorns.

Queen Anne's lace

Work the bracts with a row each of stem and outline stitch on each side. Add a colonial knot to the end of each row. Fill the centre space with three to six pistil stitches. For the flower centre, embroider a colonial knot just above the tip of the bract and pistil stitch. Work five petals around each centre in French knots *(diag 2)*.

Diag 2

For the stems, work a row of stem stitch and then a row of outline stitch side by side. Merge the two rows 1cm (3/8") from the top of the stem, leaving only stem stitch. Add single fly stitch leaves along the stem.

Wheat

Embroider the ears with bullion knots in the pale yellow thread, working one at the tip and four to five alternating pairs, 6mm (1/4") apart. Between each, work more bullion knots in the other colours.

Add whiskers by working long straight stitches between the bullion knots, extending beyond the wheat ears. Embroider the stems in stem stitch.

Work the pairs of leaves with long, narrow detached chains with long anchoring stitches, adding a straight stitch to each. Whip the stems with one strand of the rayon thread.

Dillweed and grass

Embroider the dillweed near the beehive and at the base of the toadstools. Work pistil stitch for the flowers and the stems in stem stitch. Add two pairs of fly stitch leaves. Work several small straight stitches at the base of each stem for the grass.

Toadstools

Caps

Trace the shape of the underside of the large toadstool onto the interfacing and cut out. Hand stitch the shape in place and then work blanket stitch over it *(diag 3)*.

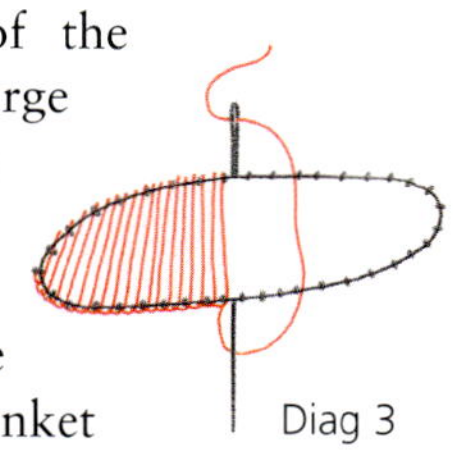

Diag 3

For the large toadstool cap, begin with the smallest felt shape and attach the three layers one on top of the other. Attach the two pieces of felt for the smaller cap in the same manner.

For the larger cap, work long and short blanket stitch along the lower edge and then one to three rows of long and short stitch, angling the stitches towards the top of the cap. Change colour and complete the cap. Embroider the smaller cap in a similar manner.

This Design Uses

Back stitch, Beading

Blanket stitch, Bullion knot

Buttonhole stitch, Colonial knot

Coral stitch, Couching

Detached chain

Double cast-on stitch

Fly stitch

Florentine stitch variation

French knot, Gathered ribbon

Granitos, Half-drop-tied stitch

Long and short blanket stitch

Long and short stitch

Needle woven picot

Oblong cross stitch

Outline stitch, Pin stitch

Pistil stitch

Portuguese knotted stem stitch

Running stitch, Satin stitch

Smocker's knot, Split back stitch

Stem stitch, Straight stitch

Trellis stitch

Twisted detached chain stitch

Whipped reverse chain stitch

Woven plait stitch

Add the spots for the large cap with colonial knots. Work French knots for the small cap.

Stalks

Attach the piece of felt for each stalk and cover with long and short stitch.

Snail

Stitch the small circle of felt for the snail shell on top of the large toadstool. Using the fine metallic thread, couch the silk in a spiral, working outwards and pulling the silk taut so that it pushes the centre upwards.

Work bullion knots for the body and tail. Embroider a colonial knot for the head and work two pistil stitches for the antennae.

Caterpillar

At the marked position on the stem, work one straight stitch using chenille thread. Couch this laid thread down with six buttonhole stitches. Use the needle to puff the chenille between the buttonhole stitches. Secure the laid thread to the back of the work using one of the fine threads. Work straight stitch spines in the metallic thread along the back of the caterpillar. Work straight stitches over the body.

Ladybirds

There are five ladybirds in the design. For the body of each, work two eight-wrap bullion knots side by side. Work a twelve-wrap bullion knot on each side. Work one black spot on each side with a six-wrap bullion knot. Stitch two more for the head. Embroider six straight stitch legs.

Web and spider

Create six spokes by working straight stitches from the centre to each marked point. Starting near the centre and taking a tiny stitch under each spoke, work five rows. At the end of the spokes, work one last row as the outline of the web.

Attach the bead for the spider with straight stitches, creating the legs.

Bees

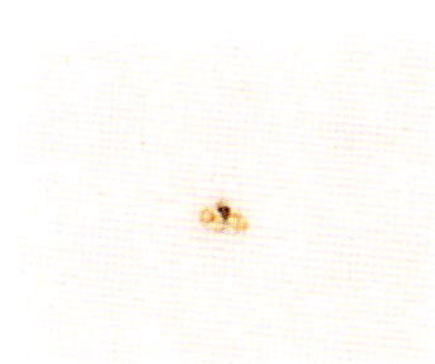

Work three colonial knots for each bee, alternating the colours. Work two detached chains for the wings.

Beehive

The beehive is worked on the *Lugana* fabric using four different needlepoint stitches. Follow the chart and the stitch diagrams on the pattern sheet. Adjust the patterns at the end of each row to accommodate the shape of the beehive.

Begin at the base of the beehive 2.5cm (1") up and across from the lower left corner of the fabric.

The lower section is worked in half-drop-tied stitch. Exclude the area for the doorway.

Work a narrow brown row in oblong cross stitch above the half-drop-tied stitch section. Work a block of Florentine stitch variation, another row of oblong cross stitch and then a block of half-drop-tied stitch. Next work a third row of oblong cross stitch and the upper section of Florentine stitch variation.

Embroider the door with vertical satin stitch.

Attaching the beehive

Machine stitch close to the outside of the embroidery. Allowing a 1cm (3/8") seam allowance, cut out the shape. Clip the seam allowance at the end of each row of oblong cross stitch. Turn the seam allowance to the wrong side and tack. Pin the beehive into position on the blanketing and hand stitch, leaving a small opening. Fill lightly with fibre-fill and hand stitch the opening closed.

Basket of flowers

Basket

Using the remaining *Lugana* fabric and following the chart on the pattern sheet, work the basket in woven plait stitch. Work a total of eighteen rows, rounding the shape of the basket at the lower corners.

Work the rim in Portuguese knotted stem stitch.

Cut the basket out allowing a 1cm (3/8") seam allowance. Fold the seam allowance to the wrong side and tack. Embroider the twisted detached chain leaves with the green silk ribbon. With one strand of the matching green silk thread, add a straight stitch to each.

The basket of flowers is positioned after the rabbit is dressed.

Flowers

Following the step-by-step instructions, make the gathered ribbon flowers.

Make four blue, three pink, three red, two yellow and two mauve flowers in the same manner, attaching them close together in a circle to form a bunch on the homespun.

Run a gathering thread around the circle of flowers. Leaving a 7mm (5/16") seam allowance, cut out the bunch of flowers. Pull up the gathering thread and secure.

Place the prepared bunch of flowers into position and stitch securely. Place the basket on the blanket and, allowing room for the fibre-fill, attach with tiny hand stitches. Leave an opening at the base. Fill with a small amount of fibre-fill and stitch the opening closed.

Handle

Work the handle in double cast-on stitch. Cut four strands of the medium hazelnut stranded silk, each 1m (40") in length. Using the darning needle, bring the strands to the front just above the rim in the centre of the upper edge of the basket. Return to the back, behind the flowers, re-emerging in the centre of the upper edge. Turn the work upside down. Divide the threads so that there are two on each side of the needle *(diag 4)*.

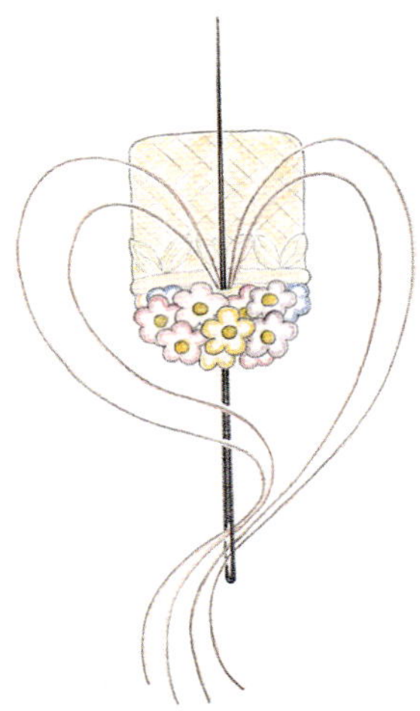

Diag 4

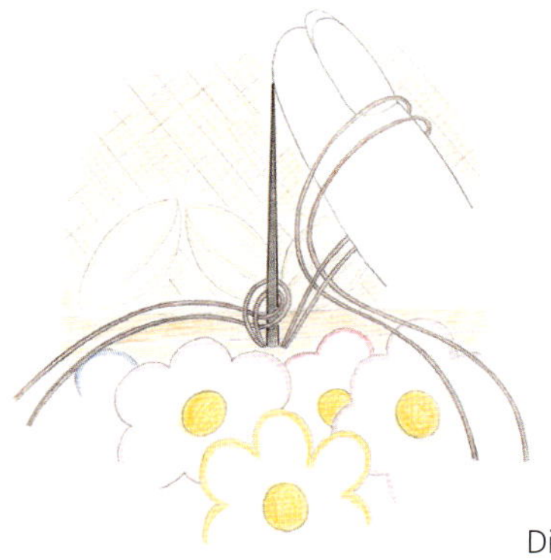

Diag 5

Cast a stitch onto the needle with the left hand thread and then with the right *(diag 5)*. Continue casting on, alternating from one side to the other, until the casting on measures 3.5cm (1 3/8"). Pull the needle carefully through the stitches, ensuring they do not twist.

When the rabbit's arm is in position, arrange the handle over it and take the threads to the back of the blanket and secure. Attach the handle to the arm with several tiny invisible stitches. Attach the tip of the paw to the blanket in the same manner.

Construction

See page 133.

Gathered Ribbon Flower

Place a 15cm (6") square of homespun into the embroidery hoop. Cut the ribbon into 10cm (4") lengths.

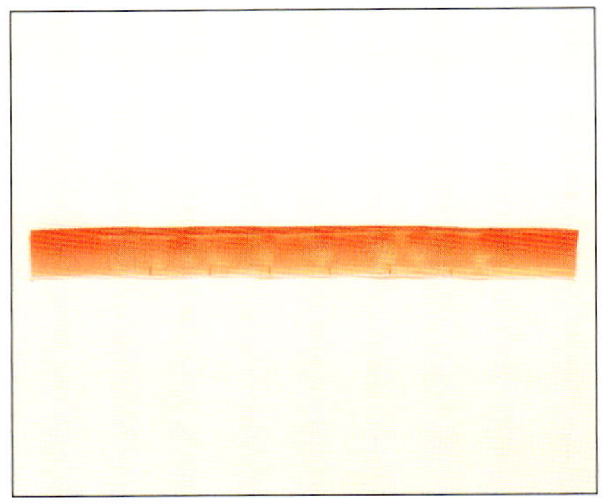

1. Mark palest edge 2.5cm (1") in from each end using a pencil. Mark distance between at 1cm (3/8") intervals.

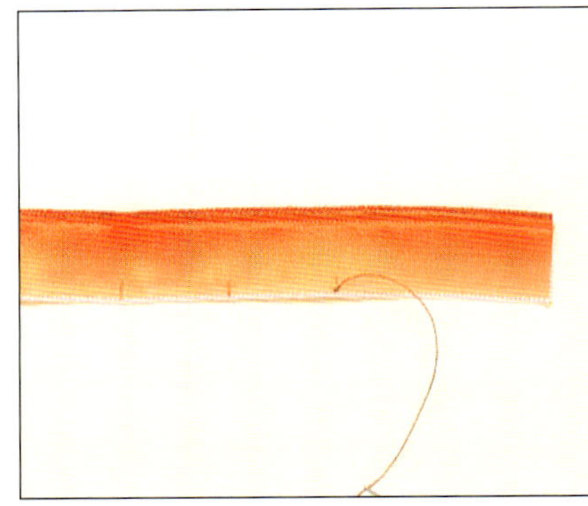

2. Knot a length of machine sewing thread and work a back stitch at the first mark.

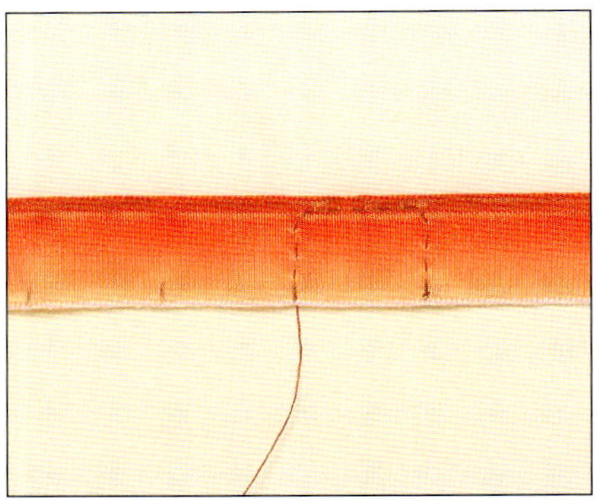

3. Work tiny running stitches up, across and down, finishing with the thread on the back.

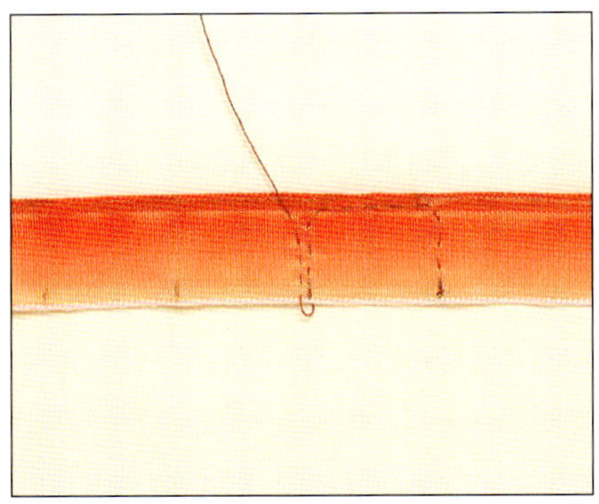

4. Bring the thread over the edge of the ribbon and stitch back towards the opposite side.

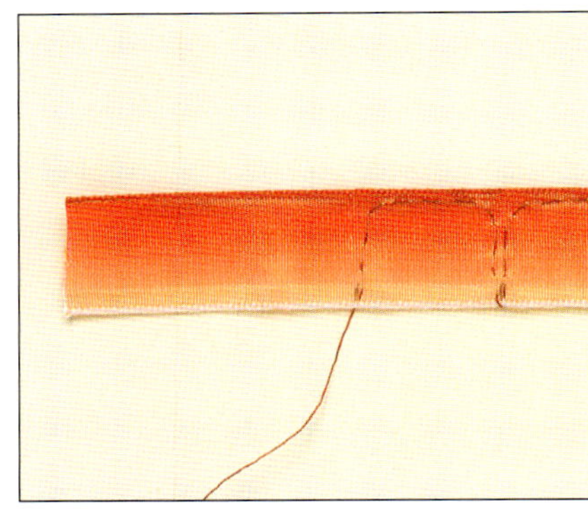

5. Continue in this manner to the last mark on the ribbon.

6. Hold the ribbon between your fingers to prevent it from twisting and pull up the running stitches firmly.

7. Secure thread but do not cut it. Bring two ends of the stitching together. Take thread through the starting knot.

8. Attaching the flower. Place the large chenille needle in the fabric. Thread the tails of ribbon into the needle.

9. Pull tails to back of fabric. Remove the needle. Trim the tails at an angle. Use the dangling thread to secure the tails. Bring the thread to the front.

10. Secure the flower with tiny stab stitches in the folds of ribbon close to the centre.

11. Work a French knot at the centre of the flower.

Threads, Ribbons, Beads and Needles

DMC stranded cotton
A = 680 dk old gold
B = 729 med old gold
C = 762 vy lt pearl grey
D = 921 copper
E = 3051 dk green-grey
F = 3371 black-brown
G = 3721 dk shell pink

Gumnut Yarns 'Stars' stranded silk
H = 645 med khaki
I = 646 med dk khaki
J = 744 med lt daffodil
K = 746 med dk daffodil
L = 850 palest salmon pink
M = 857 dk salmon pink
N = 859 ultra dk salmon pink
O = 943 lt hazelnut
P = 945 med hazelnut
Q = 947 dk hazelnut
R = 991 ecru

Gumnut Yarns 'Buds' perlé silk
S = 645 med khaki

Gumnut Yarns 'Daisies' fine wool
T = 010 palest watermelon
U = 013 lt watermelon
V = 093 lt raspberry
W = 645 med khaki
X = 646 med dk khaki
Y = 746 med dk daffodil
Z = 991 ecru
AA = 992 vy lt pewter
AB = 994 med lt pewter
AC = 998 vy dk pewter

Gumnut Yarns 'Blossoms' crewel wool
AD = 010 palest watermelon
AE = 012 vy lt watermelon
AF = 153 lt cherry brandy
AG = 155 med cherry brandy

Gumnut Yarns 'Tulips' mohair
AH = 645 med khaki

Gumnut Yarns 'Moonbeams' variegated mohair
AI = dk topaz

Gumnut Yarns 'Opals' wool and silk
AJ = dk topaz

Needlepaints stranded cotton
AK = 2001 vy lt lavender blue
AL = 2002 lt lavender blue
AM = 2003 lavender blue
AN = 2005 dk lavender blue

Needlepoint 8 ply silk
AO = 221 ultra lt berry red
AP = 222 vy lt berry red
AQ = 224 berry red

Madeira stranded silk
AR = 2400 black
AS = 2401 soft white
AT = 2014 ultra lt tan

Rajmahal stranded rayon
AU = 311 fresco oil
AV = 841 gilded bronze

YLI silk floss
AW = 181 gold beige
AX = 821 raspberry

YLI 1000 denier silk
AY = 39 lt Jacobean green

YLI 380 denier silk
AZ = white

YLI 601 fine metallic
BA = 1 gold

Minnamurra stranded cotton
BB = 200 beige

Kacoonda hi-twist silk
BC = 6c autumn rose
BD = 106 antique green

Kacoonda fine silk
BE = 106 antique green

Colour Streams 'Silken Strands' stranded silk
BF = 18 antique ivory
BG = 36 saltbush

The Thread Gatherer Sheep's Silk
BH = 057 moss green
BI = 068 dark moss
BJ = 087 aqua clouds

DMC Broder Médicis wool
BK = 8412 avocado

DMC stranded rayon
BL = 30543 beige

Au ver à Soie Chenille à broder
BM = 2124 green

Au Ver à Soie Antique Metallics
BN = 210 brown-black
BO = 520 copper

French Elegance Ribbon Ombre

Faveur variegated ribbon 4mm (3/16") wide
BP = 40cm (16") no. 3 blue
BQ = 20cm (8") no. 4 yellow
BR = 30cm (12") no. 12 red
BS = 20cm (8") no. 16 mauve
BT = 30cm (12") no. 18 pink

YLI silk ribbon 2mm (1/8") wide
BU = 30cm (12") no. 32 pistachio green

Mill Hill glass seed beads
BV = 00206 violet
BW = 02024 heather mauve

Maria George Delica beads
BX = DBR 464 galvanized dark purple

Irridescent AB bead 2mm (1/8") wide
BY = black (1 bead)

Fine heirloom sewing thread
BZ = white

Needles
No. 5 crewel needle
No. 8 crewel needle
No. 10 crewel needle
No. 12 crewel needle
No. 8 milliner's needle
No. 9 milliner's needle
No. 10 milliner's needle
No. 24 tapestry needle
No. 26 tapestry needle
No. 28 tapestry needle
No. 18 chenille needle
No. 22 chenille needle
No. 7 long darner needle

Embroidery Key

All embroidery is worked with one strand unless otherwise specified.

Head

Eye

Outline = AR (split back stitch), 10 crewel

White section = AS (satin stitch), 10 crewel

Pupil = AR (satin stitch), 10 crewel

Face = AA and BJ (long and short stitch), 5 crewel

Nose = U (satin stitch), 5 crewel

Mouth = AC (split back stitch), 5 crewel

Whiskers = BN (straight stitch), 10 crewel

Attached ear = BJ (long and short stitch), 5 crewel

Detached ear

Front = T, U, Z, AA and AB (long and short stitch), 5 crewel

Back = AB (long and short stitch), 5 crewel

Feet = BJ (long and short stitch), 5 crewel

Paw = AB (long and short stitch), 5 crewel

Skirt = AZ (coral stitch, stem stitch), 10 crewel

Apron = BZ (running stitch), 12 crewel, (pin stitch), 28 tapestry

Wild roses

Flowers

Petals = AD (2 strands, granitos), 22 chenille

Petal tip highlights = V (straight stitch, fly stitch), 5 crewel

Between petals = BK (straight stitch), 5 crewel

Petal inner highlights = AX (straight stitch), 10 crewel

Centre = D, E, G and Y (1 strand of each blended together, colonial knot), 5 crewel

Small rosebuds

Petals = AD or AE (2 strands, granitos, straight stitch), 22 chenille

Petal tip highlights = V (fly stitch, straight stitch), 5 crewel

Bud tip = H (fly stitch, straight stitch), 10 crewel

Calyx = H, W, X, BG and BH (straight stitch), 5 crewel

Stems = W, X or BH (laid thread, couching), 5 crewel, H and BG (whipping), 26 tapestry

Large rosebud

Petals = AG (granitos, straight stitch), AF then AE (2 strands, granitos), 18 chenille

Calyx = H and X (straight stitch), 10 crewel

Bud tip = H (fly stitch), 10 crewel

Stem = X (laid thread, couching), 5 crewel, H and BC (whipping), 26 tapestry

Rosehips

Hips = AQ (long and short stitch), 10 crewel

Highlights = AO, AP (long and short stitch), BO (straight stitch), 10 crewel

Tip = BN (pistil stitch), 10 crewel

Stems = W (reverse chain), 5 crewel, I (whipping), 26 tapestry or BD (laid thread), BE (couching), 5 crewel, H (whipping), 26 tapestry

Leaves = AH, AI, AJ, BE, BG, BH and BI (fly stitch, smocker's knot), 5 crewel

Blackberries

Berries

Darkest berry = AN (2 strands, trellis stitch), 26 tapestry, AM (2 strands, bullion loop, 10 - 12 wraps), BX (beading), 9 milliner's

Medium berry = AM (2 strands, trellis stitch), 26 tapestry, AL (2 strands, bullion loop, 10 - 12 wraps), BV (beading), 9 milliner's

Lightest berry = AL (2 strands, trellis stitch), 26 tapestry, AK (2 strands, bullion loop, 10 - 12 wraps), BW (beading), 9 milliner's

Sepals = AY (needlewoven picot), 24 tapestry

Stems = BE (2 strands, whipped reverse chain stitch), 26 tapestry

Thorns = BE (fly stitch), 10 crewel

Leaves = BG (2 strands, fly stitch, smocker's knot), AH, AI and AJ (fly stitch, smocker's knot), 5 crewel

Spent blackberry flowers

Stamens = BB (straight stitch), AV (French knot, 1 wrap), AT or BL (2 strands, colonial knot), 8 crewel

Sepals = H (fly stitch), 10 crewel

Stem = BE (whipped reverse chain stitch), 10 crewel, 26 tapestry

Queen Anne's lace

Bract = H (stem stitch or outline stitch, colonial knot, pistil stitch), 10 crewel

Flower centre = AW (3 strands, colonial knot), 8 crewel

Petals = BF (2 strands, French knot, 1 or 2 wraps), 5 crewel

Stem = H or S (1 strand, stem stitch, outline stitch), 10 crewel

Leaves = H (fly stitch), 10 crewel

Wheat

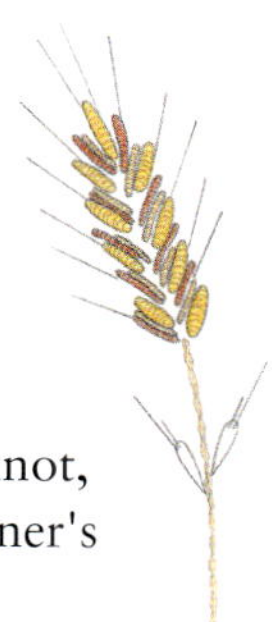

Ears = J (3 strands, bullion knot, 10 wraps), AW (3 strands, bullion knot, 12 - 14 wraps), O (2 strands, bullion knot, 12 - 14 wraps), 8 milliner's

Whiskers = AU (straight stitch), 10 crewel

Stem = O (stem stitch), 10 crewel, AU (whipping), 26 tapestry

Leaves = O (detached chain), AU (1 strand, straight stitch), 10 crewel

Dillweed and grass

Flowers = BE (pistil stitch), 10 crewel

Stems = BE (stem stitch), 10 crewel

Leaves = BE (fly stitch), 10 crewel

Grass = BE (straight stitch), 10 crewel

Toadstools

Large toadstool

Underside = L (blanket stitch), 10 crewel

Cap = N (long and short blanket stitch, long and short stitch), M (long and short stitch), 10 crewel

Spots = R (3 strands, colonial knot), 5 crewel

Stalk = O and R (long and short stitch), 10 crewel

Small toadstool

Cap = N (long and short blanket stitch, long and short stitch), 10 crewel

Spots = L (3 strands, French knot, 1 wrap), 5 crewel

Stalk = O and R (long and short stitch), 10 crewel

Snail

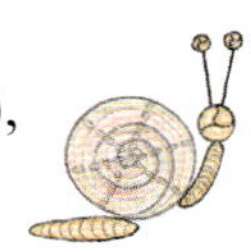

Shell = BC (laid thread), BA (couching), 10 crewel

Body = BB (2 strands, bullion knot, 12 wraps), 10 milliner's

Tail = BB (2 strands, bullion knot, 10 wraps), 10 milliner's

Head = BB (2 strands, colonial knot), 10 milliner's

Antennae = BB (pistil stitch), 10 milliner's

Caterpillar

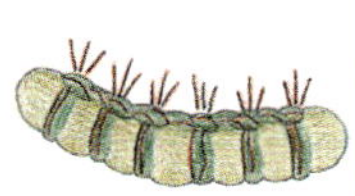

Body = BM (laid thread), 18 chenille, 3 strands of BG with 1 strand of BO (buttonhole stitch), 8 crewel

Markings = BO (straight stitch, couching), 10 crewel

Ladybirds

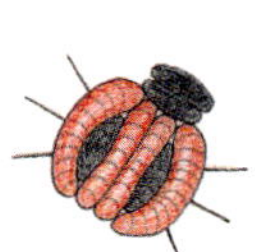

Body = N (2 strands, 4 bullion knots, 8 or 12 wraps), 9 milliner's

Spots = AR (2 bullion knots, 6 wraps), 9 milliner's

Head = AR (2 bullion knots, 6 wraps), 9 milliner's

Legs = BN (straight stitch), 10 crewel

Web and spider

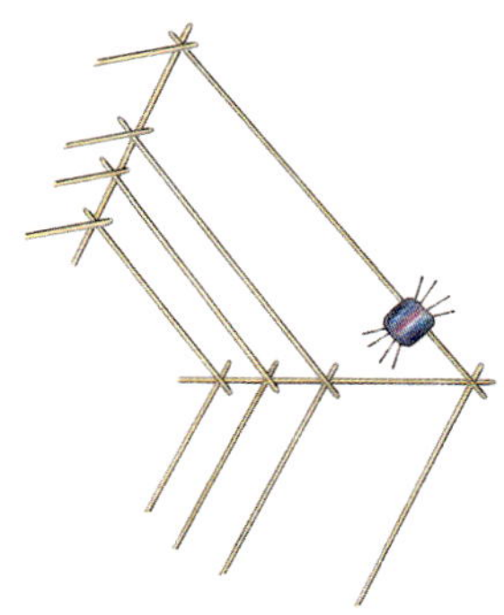

Web = BA (straight stitch), 10 crewel

Spider = BY and AN (straight stitch), 10 crewel

Bees

Body = F and B (3 strands, colonial knot), 8 crewel

Wings = C (detached chain), 10 crewel

Beehive

Wall = K (3 strands, half-drop-tied stitch, Florentine stitch variation), Q (2 strands, oblong cross stitch), 26 tapestry

Doorway = Q (3 strands, satin stitch), 26 tapestry

Basket of flowers

Basket = P (3 strands, Portuguese knotted stem stitch, woven plait stitch), 26 tapestry

Flowers = BP, BQ, BR, BS and BT (gathered ribbon), 10 crewel

Flower centres = AW (6 strands, French knot, 1 wrap) or A (4 strands, French knot, 1 wrap), 5 crewel

Leaves = BU (twisted detached chain stitch), 24 tapestry, BG (straight stitch), 10 crewel

Handle = P (4 strands, double cast-on stitch), 7 long darner

WORKING *the* RABBIT HEAD

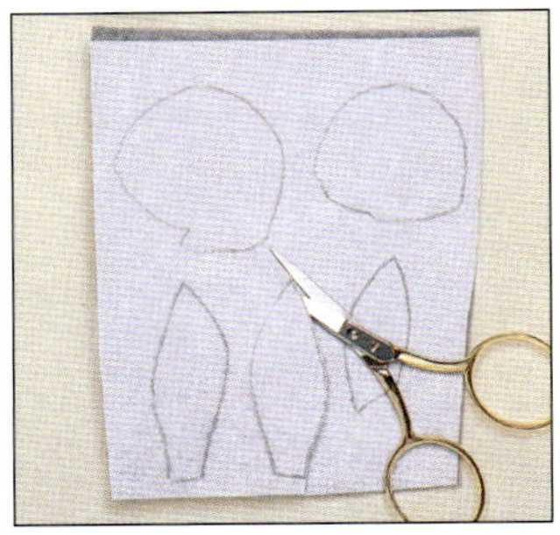

1. Padding. Trace the shapes onto the smooth side of the appliqué paper. Fuse to the grey felt and cut out.

2. Peel off the backing paper. Using small stitches, attach the smaller head shape.

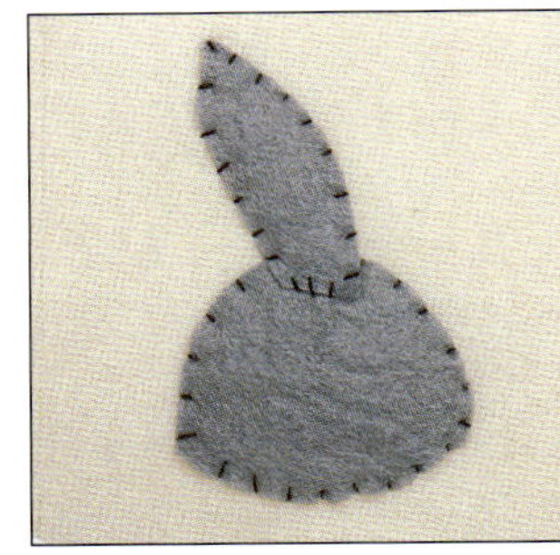

3. Place the rabbit's left ear in position and attach over the smaller head shape.

4. Place the remaining head shape over the top and stitch in place.

5. Eye. Outline the eye and then work the white section. Work several layers in black for the pupil.

6. Face. Referring to stitch direction diagram, work the guidelines for stitch placement with grey wool.

7. Referring to the close up photograph, work the grey area of the face in long and short stitch.

8. Nose. Embroider the nose with several satin stitches worked on top of each other.

9. Mouth and whiskers. Work split back stitch for the mouth. Add straight stitches for the whiskers.

10. Attached ear. Cover the felt with long and short stitches. Start at the base and work towards the tip.

11. Detached ear. With glue sides facing, overcast the two shapes together. Leave the lower edge open.

12. Beginning at lower edge, work long and short stitch through the top layer only to cover front of ear.

13. Completely cover the back of the ear with long and short stitches in the same manner as the front.

14. Attaching the ear. Fold the ear in half lengthwise. Stitch at the lower edge so the ear 'cups'.

15. Hand stitch the rabbit's ear in position.

BLACKBERRY

When covering the padding with trellis stitch, refer to the stitch glossary on page 126. Work from left to right, then from right to left, increasing and decreasing as required.

On the project, the sepals are worked at the base of the blackberry. For clarity, we have shown the sepals worked in isolation.

Trace two blackberry shapes for each berry onto the appliqué paper. Fuse to the grey felt and cut out. Peel off the backing paper.

1. With the glue side up, hand stitch the small shape and then the large one to the blanket.

2. Work six small back stitches along the top of the berry close to the felt.

3. Trellis stitch. Work a row of trellis stitch along the row of back stitch

4. Anchoring at each end of the rows, work trellis stitch to cover the shape.

5. Cover the berry with bullion loops. Work 12 wraps for the middle loops, and 10 wraps for the others.

6. Attach 8 or 9 beads with the *Nymo* thread between the loops.

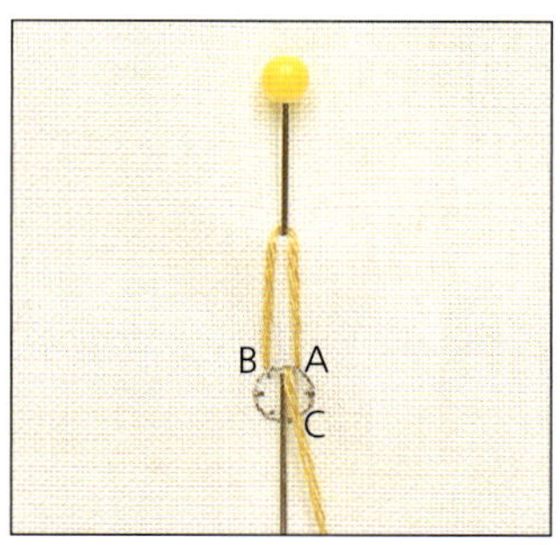

7. Sepals. Insert a pin. Bring the thread to the front and wrap around the pin from A to B. Emerge at C.

8. Wrap the thread around the head of the pin in a clockwise direction.

9. Weave the needle from right to left under, over, and under the threads.

10. Pull the thread through. Weave the needle from left to right, over, under and over the threads.

11. Continue weaving to the base, keeping the tension even and packing the weaving tightly.

12. Take the working thread to the back and secure. Remove the pin.

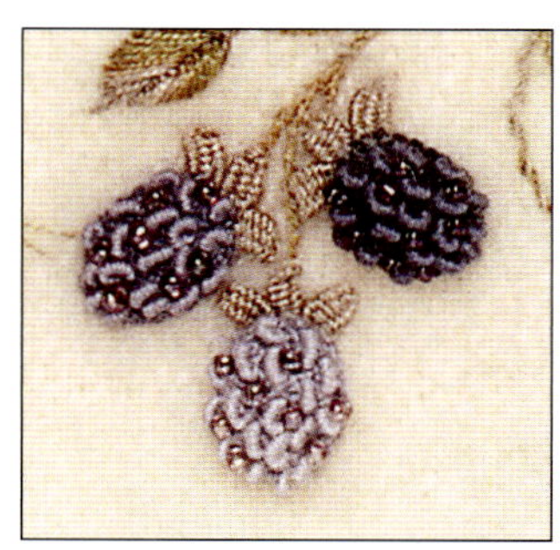

13. Work two more sepals, attaching the tips so that the sepals arch slightly.

THE FINISHED BLANKET MEASURES 110CM X 82CM WIDE (44" X 32")

Delicate sprays of softly coloured flowers,

enveloped between dainty scrolls, decorate the ends of this soft ivory wool blanket. Tiny nosegays embellish each corner. Stem stitch borders of blue-violet provide a framework for roses, daisies and lavender. Soft cream twill forms the backing and edges of the blanket.

REQUIREMENTS

Fabric

110cm x 82cm wide (43" x 32") piece of ivory wool blanketing

122cm x 94cm wide (48" x 37") piece of cream polycotton twill

Supplies

Tracing paper

Water-soluble fabric marker

Sharp HB pencil

Threads and needle

See page 113.

PREPARATION FOR EMBROIDERY

See page 134 for the placement of the borders and the pattern sheet for the embroidery designs.

THIS DESIGN USES

Back stitch, Bullion knot

Bullion loop, Detached chain

Fly stitch, French knot

Granitos, Stem stitch

• • •

Transferring the sprays and posies

Trace the flower sprays, including the border placement marks onto tracing paper using the HB pencil. Matching placement marks with the previously worked stem stitch border, centre and pin the large spray design in position on one short end. Using the needle, pierce holes in the paper at the centre of each rose and daisy and several holes along the lavender stems and scrolls. Mark through the holes with the fabric marker. Remove the tracing and join the dots along each stem and scroll to make continuous lines. Repeat for the remaining spray on the opposite end.

Transfer the posies to each corner of the blanket in the same manner, turning and mirroring as necessary.

Every breath of air and ray of light and heat,
every beautiful prospect, is, as it were, the skirts of their garments,
the waving of the robes of those whose faces see God.

John Henry Newman

Embroidery

Order of work

Borders

Stitch the borders with stem stitch. At each corner take the thread to the back of the work. Slide the needle under the back of the last stitch worked *(diag 1)*.

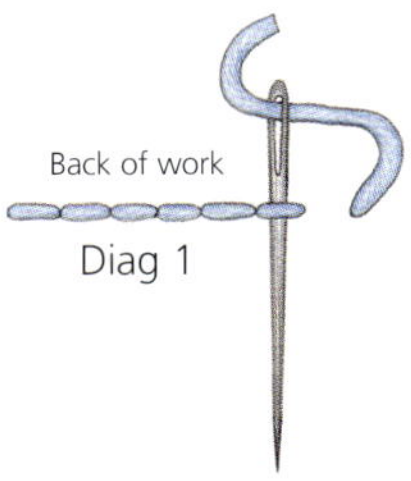

Diag 1

Diag 2

Re-emerge at the corner through the same hole *(diag 2)*. Continue working stem stitch down the next side. This ensures sharp, right angled corners *(diag 3)*.

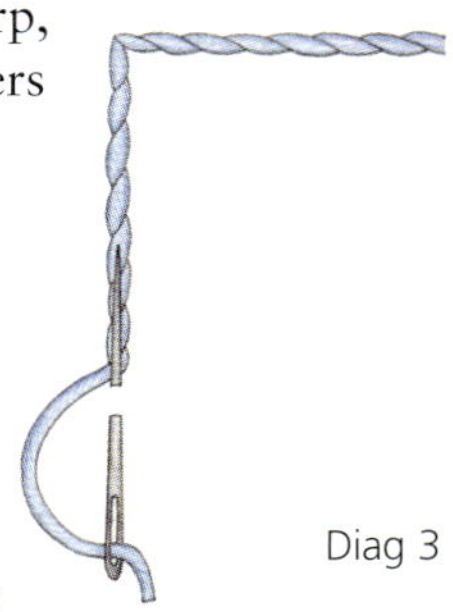

Diag 3

Floral spray

Roses

Embroider the bullion roses, beginning each with a bullion loop centre. Add three bullion knots for the inner petals. Work the outer petals with five bullion knots for the central rose and two for each of the side roses. Add the calyx to each rose with two fly stitches. Work two detached chain stitches on each side of the central rose for leaves.

White daisies and buds

Stitch the three white daisies with eight detached chain stitch petals and the partial daisy with four. Add a French knot to the centre of each.

Stitch a bud at each end of the spray with two petals for each bud. Work a fly stitch around the base.

Blue daisies and buds

Work these in a similar manner to the white daisies, with six petals for the full flowers. Stitch three to five petals for the partial flowers and two petals for the buds.

Pink daisies

Embroider the pink daisy with five granitos petals. Work each granitos with four stitches. Add a French knot centre. Stitch the partial daisies with two or three petals.

Lavender

Embroider a detached chain stitch for each lavender flower. Work a straight stitch inside each chain stitch using the darker shade of mauve. Add a fly stitch calyx at the base of the top flower and around the base of each pair. The anchor stitch of each fly stitch forms the stem.

Foliage

Work the foliage among the spray in detached chain stitch, fly stitch and French knots.

Scrolls

Stitch the blue scrolls in back stitch.

Blue dots

Work a French knot at the outermost point on each end of the spray.

Posies

Embroider the rose, blue daisy and partial white daisy in a similar manner to those in the spray. When stitching the rose, work two bullion knots for the inner petals and three bullion knots for the outer petals. Add a stem with back stitch.

Construction

See page 134.

THREADS *and* NEEDLE

Appleton 2 ply crewel wool

A = 353 lt grey-green
B = 461 vy lt cornflower (3 skeins)
C = 552 lt bright yellow
D = 601 ultra lt mauve
E = 603 lt mauve
F = 751 ultra lt rose pink
G = 754 lt rose pink
H = 755 rose pink
I = 992 off-white

Needle

No. 20 chenille needle

EMBROIDERY KEY

All embroidery is worked with two strands unless otherwise specified.

Border = B (1 strand, stem stitch)

Large rose in spray

Centre = H (bullion loop, 10 wraps)
Inner petals = G (3 bullion knots, 10 wraps)
Outer petals = F (5 bullion knots, 14 wraps)
Calyx = A (1 strand, fly stitch)
Leaves = A (1 strand, detached chain)

Small rose in spray

Centre = H (bullion loop, 10 wraps)
Inner petals = G (3 bullion knots, 10 wraps)
Outer petals = F (2 bullion knots, 14 wraps)
Calyx = A (1 strand, fly stitch)

Rose in posy

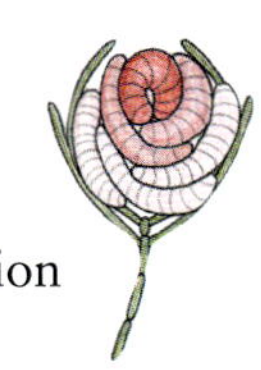

Centre = H (bullion loop, 10 wraps)
Inner petals = G (2 bullion knots, 10 wraps)
Outer petals = F (3 bullion knots, 14 wraps)
Calyx = A (1 strand, fly stitch)
Stem = A (1 strand, back stitch, detached chain, French knot, 1 wrap)

White daisies and buds

Petals = I (detached chain)
Centre = C (French knot, 1 wrap)

Foliage on bud = A (1 strand, fly stitch)

Blue daisies and buds

Petals = B (detached chain)
Centre = C (French knot, 1 wrap)
Foliage on bud = A (1 strand, fly stitch)

Pink daisies

Petals = F (granitos)
Centre = I (French knot, 1 wrap)

Lavender

Flowers = D (1 strand, detached chain) and E (1 strand, straight stitch)
Calyx and stems = A (1 strand, fly stitch)

Foliage = A (1 strand, detached chain, fly stitch, French knot, 1 or 2 wraps)

Scrolls = B (back stitch)

Blue dots = B (1 strand, French knot, 1 wrap)

The GUIDES of FAIRLEY
WARNE'S HAPPY BOOK FOR GIRLS
FULLY ILLUSTRATED

The warm, earthly tones of the blanket fabric create a perfect background for the threadpainted piglet and geese. The unique picnic bag is made from matching check fabric with an insertion of green hessian. Stitched on the hessian are three inquisitive geese peeping over a brick wall.

Requirements for picnic blanket

The requirements for the framed effect on the blanket will depend on your choice of fabrics. See pages 131 and 132 for instructions for calculating fabric and piping amounts.

Fabric

85cm x 50cm wide (34" x 20") piece of brown wool blanketing

Brown cotton fabric for framing and backing the blanket

Check fabric for framing the blanket

Supplies

Thin wadding

Golden maize satin mini piping

30cm (12") quilting hoop

White tissue paper

Sharp HB pencil

This Design Uses

Back stitch, Detached chain

Fly stitch, French knot

Interlocked straight stitch

Satin stitch, Straight stitch

Requirements for bag

65cm x 100cm wide (26" x 40") piece of check fabric

40cm (16") square of green hessian

55cm x 90cm wide (22" x 36") piece of polyester lining

Supplies

25cm x 35cm wide (10" x 14") piece of grey lightweight fusible interfacing

1.7m (1 yd 31") olive green rayon lacing cord

1.1m (1yd 8") size 7 piping cord

1 metre (40") golden maize satin mini piping

20cm (8") quilting hoop

White tissue paper

Sharp HB pencil

Threads & Needles

See page 122.

Busy Bodies Picnic Rug

Preparation for Embroidery

See the pattern sheet for the embroidery designs and the stitch direction diagrams.

Preparing the fabrics

Blanket

Fold the blanketing in half across the width. Using pale machine sewing thread, stitch a row of tacking along the fold line. Refold the fabric along the length. Tack along the fold line.

Bag

Fuse the piece of interfacing onto one side of the hessian. Fold the hessian and work rows of tacking in the same manner as the rug.

Transferring the designs

Blanket

Using the pencil, trace the blanket embroidery design, including the placement marks, onto the tissue paper. Position the tracing onto the right side of the blanketing, aligning the placement marks with the lines of tacking. Pin the tracing in place.

Using contrasting sewing thread and small tacking stitches, tack through the tissue paper and the blanketing along the design lines. Most tacking threads marking the design can remain in the work permanently as the embroidery will cover them. Lightly moisten the tissue paper with a damp sponge, wait a few seconds, then carefully remove the paper.

Bag

Using contrasting sewing thread, transfer the bag design onto the hessian in the same manner.

Embroidery

Stitch the embroidery with the fabric in the hoop, except when working the detached chain stitch and fly stitch.

Use the crewel needle for stitching with the stranded threads and the chenille needle for all remaining threads. Follow the stitch direction diagrams for placing the stitches and refer to the photographs for colour changes throughout the designs.

Order of work

Blanket

Piglet

Work the face, body and legs in shades of pink, beige and brown. Stitch the outlining at the neck and along the lower back.

Embroider the ears in a similar manner, carefully noting the colour and placement of the outlining. Work tiny hairs on the ear to the left of the design using the ecru thread.

Work the trotters, noting that a different textured thread is used.

Embroider the eye in black once the pink stitches of the skin are worked.

Stitch the end of the snout, adding the details in black, then embroider the mouth.

Geese

Embroider the feathers in white and grey thread, then work the outlining around the feathers using the darker shades of threads.

Embroider the eyes after stitching the feathers.

Stitch the beaks and feet using orange shades and then add their outlines.

Wall

Embroider the bricks with stitches placed horizontally. Work the outlines in the darker thread.

Foliage and flowers

Work small areas of grass and leaves at the base of the wall after stitching the animals.

Embroider the shrubs that appear over the wall, using both the light and dark shades of the yarns.

Work the yellow daisies with a detached chain stitch for each petal. Add a smaller detached chain stitch inside the first. Embroider the purple crocuses and the scattered blue and mauve flowers.

Bag

Geese, wall and flowers

Work these in a similar manner to those on the blanket, noting the change in threads. When working the beaks, stitch with the daffodil thread first, then overlay with the dark peach melba thread.

Lettering

Form the letters beginning with the lines and curves, then add the French knots for the dots and serifs.

Construction

See pages 134 - 137.

J.McW. '02

Busy Bodies Picnic Rug

Threads and Needles

The following threads are the requirements for both projects.

For the rug only, select all threads except AI, AO and AQ.

For the bag only, select A, B, D, L, M, N, P, Q, R, S, T, V, AI, AK, AO and AQ.

DMC stranded cotton

A = 310 black

Rajmahal stranded rayon

B = 25 Lagerfeld ink

Gumnut Yarns 'Daisies' fine wool

C = 273 lt hyacinth

D = 275 med hyacinth

E = 277 dk hyacinth

F = 297 dk lavender

G = 299 ultra dk lavender

H = 386 med dk cornflower

I = 389 ultra dk cornflower

J = 545 med forest grove

K = 648 vy dk khaki

L = 679 ultra dark olive

M = 708 vy dk lemon crush

N = 748 vy dk daffodil

O = 785 med apricot delight

P = 945 med hazelnut

Q = 947 dk hazelnut

R = 949 ultra dk hazelnut

S = 967 dk chocolate dip

T = 990 white

U = 992 vy lt pewter

V = 998 vy dk pewter

W = 999 nearly black

Gumnut Yarns 'Poppies' silk and wool

X = 780 palest apricot delight

Y = 782 vy lt apricot delight

Z = 853 lt salmon pink

AA = 855 med salmon pink

AB = 863 lt flesh

AC = 865 med flesh

AD = 867 dk flesh

AE = 943 lt hazelnut

AF = 966 med dk chocolate dip

AG = 990 white

AH = 994 med lt pewter

Gumnut Yarns 'Stars' stranded silk

AI = 746 med dk daffodil

AJ = 825 med peach melba

AK = 827 dk peach melba

AL = 869 ultra dk flesh

AM = 945 med hazelnut

AN = 949 ultra dk hazelnut

AO = 990 white

AP = 991 ecru

AQ = 992 vy lt pewter

Needles

No. 9 crewel needle

No. 22 chenille needle

The finished bag measures 56cm high x 19cm in diameter (22" x 7 1/2").

The finished blanket measures 122cm x 87cm wide (48" x 34").

~ EMBROIDERY KEY ~

All embroidery is worked with one strand unless otherwise specified.

Blanket

Piglet

Face, body and legs = X, Y, AB, AC, AD, AE, AF (interlocked straight stitch)

Neck and back outline = A, V and Y (straight stitch)

Ears = Z, AA, AC, AD, AE and AG (interlocked straight stitch), AG and AH (straight stitch)

Trotters = AL, AM, AN and AP (satin stitch, interlocked straight stitch), A and AH (straight stitch)

Eye = A (2 strands, straight stitch, back stitch, satin stitch)

Eyebrow = A (2 strands, straight stitch)

End of snout = A, X, AC, AG and AH (straight stitch), A (back stitch, satin stitch)

Mouth = A (back stitch)

Geese

Feathers = T and U (interlocked straight stitch), A or B and W (straight stitch, back stitch)

Beaks

Beak = AK (interlocked straight stitch), A and B (back stitch)

Inside of open beak = AJ (satin stitch)

Eyes = A (back stitch, 3 strands, French knot, 2 wraps)

Feet

Foot at far left = AJ (interlocked straight stitch), B (back stitch)

Remaining feet = AK (interlocked straight stitch), B (back stitch, straight stitch)

Wall

Bricks = P, Q, R and S (interlocked straight stitch)

Outlines = V (straight stitch, back stitch)

Foliage

Grass = L (straight stitch)

Leaves = J and L (detached chain)

Shrub leaf = K (fly stitch, straight stitch)

Flowers

Yellow daisies

Petals = M or N (detached chain stitch)

Centres = O (French knot, 2 - 3 wraps)

Purple crocuses = C, D and E (detached chain)

Blue flowers = H and I (detached chain)

Mauve flowers = F and G (French knot, 2 - 3 wraps)

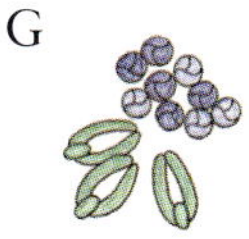

Bag

Geese

Feathers = AO and AQ (interlocked straight stitch) A and B (back stitch)

Beaks = AI and AK (interlocked straight stitch), B (back stitch)

Eyes = A (back stitch, 3 strands, French knot, 2 wraps)

Wall

Bricks = P, Q, R and S (interlocked straight stitch)

Outlines = V (straight stitch, back stitch)

Foliage = L (fly stitch, straight stitch)

Flowers

Yellow daisies

Petals = M (detached chain)

Centres = N (French knot, 2 - 3 wraps)

Purple daisies

Petals = D (French knot, 2 - 3 wraps)

Centres = T (French knot, 2 - 3 wraps)

Yellow buds = M (French knot, 2 - 3 wraps)

Lettering = A (2 strands, back stitch, straight stitch, French knot, 2 - 3 wraps)

Signing your masterpiece

Just as painters sign their work, anyone who creates a piece of art through embroidery should be proud to sign and date their work as Jenny McWhinney has done on this blanket. These details, which will be invaluable to future generations, can be incorporated into the design and colour scheme.

Stitch Glossary

Back Stitch

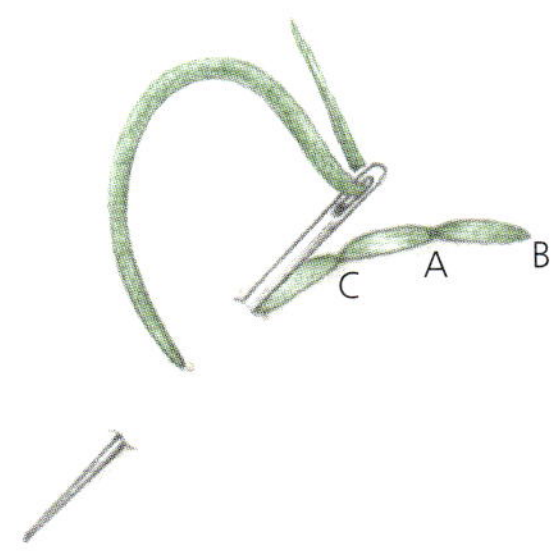

Blanket Stitch

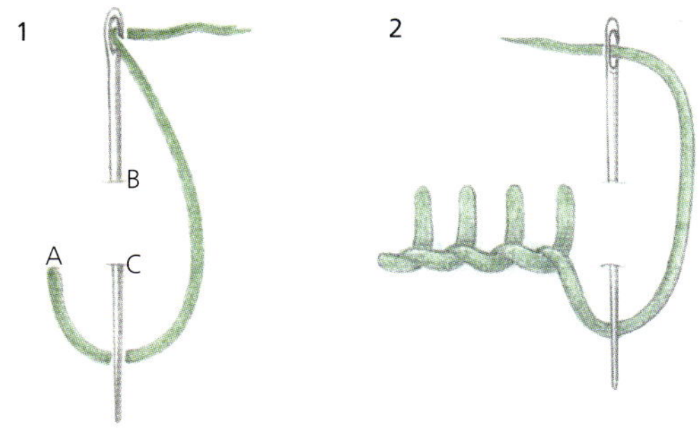

Buttonhole Stitch

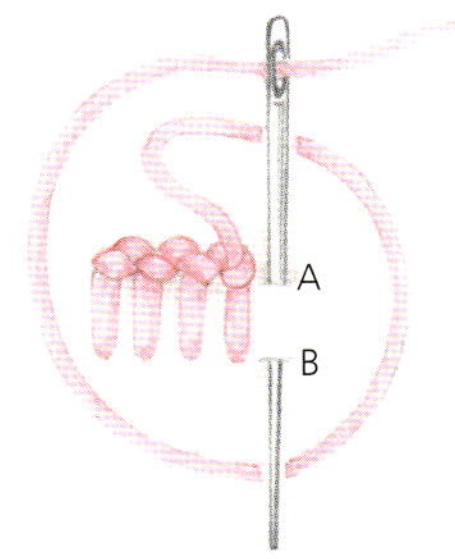

Bullion Knot

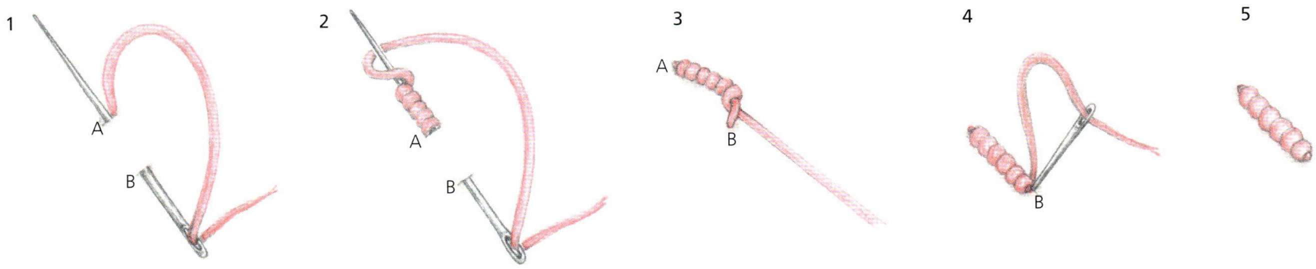

Bring thread to front at A. Pick up fabric the required length of the finished knot.

Wind enough wraps around needle to cover required distance.

Holding wraps, pull needle through.

Insert needle at B.

Bullion Loop

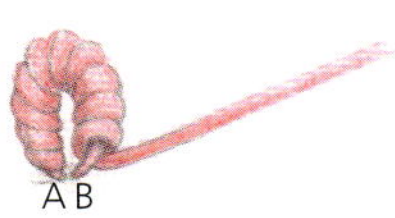

A loop is formed when A and B are very close and many wraps are used.

Chain Stitch

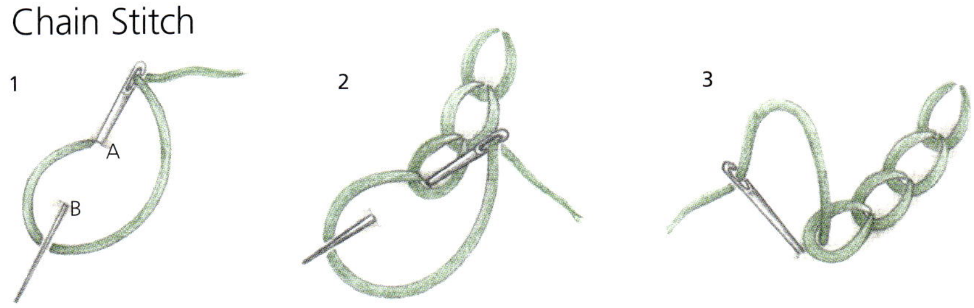

Colonial Knot

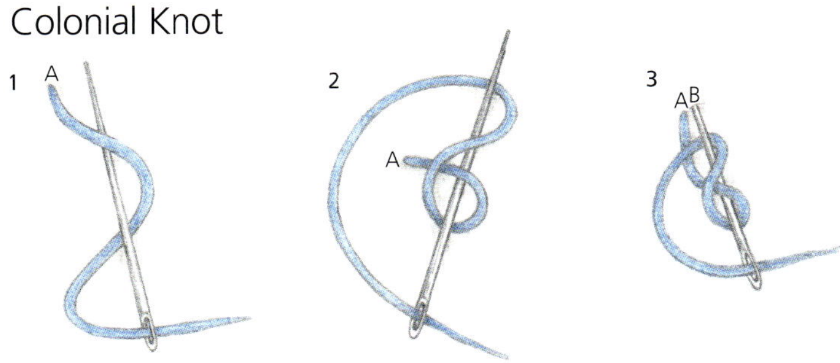

Coral Stitch

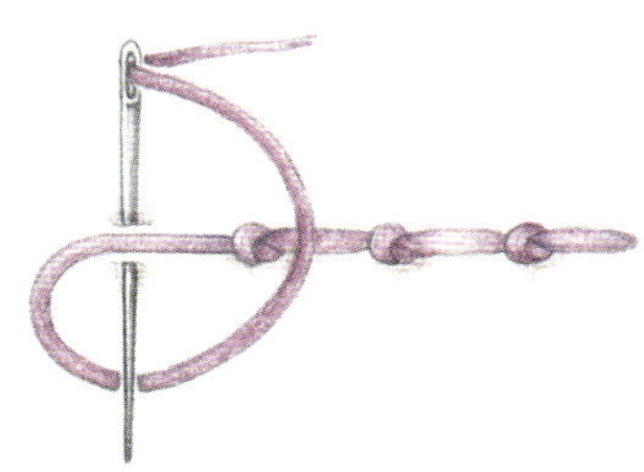

Couching

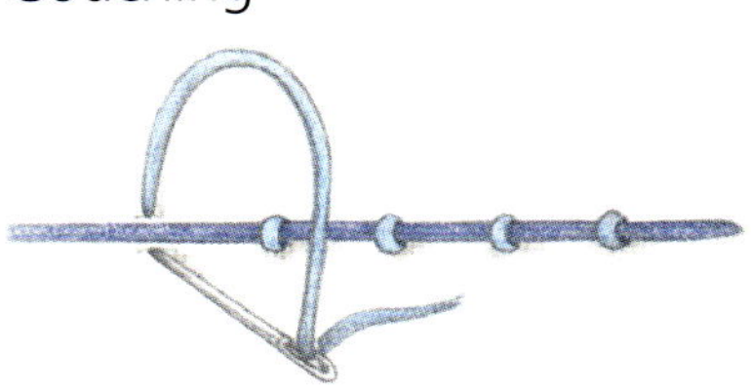

Laid thread is attached using a second thread.

Detached Blanket Stitch

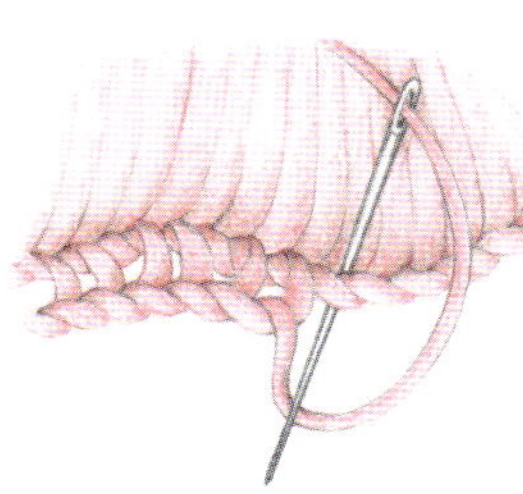

Work the detached stitches into some or all of the loops formed by previously worked blanket stitch.

Detached Chain

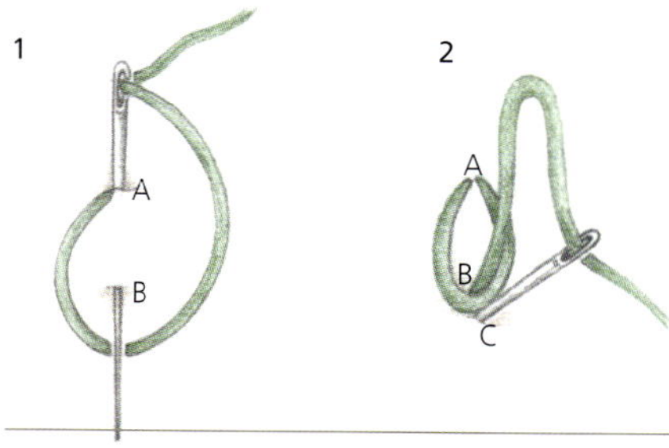

French Knot

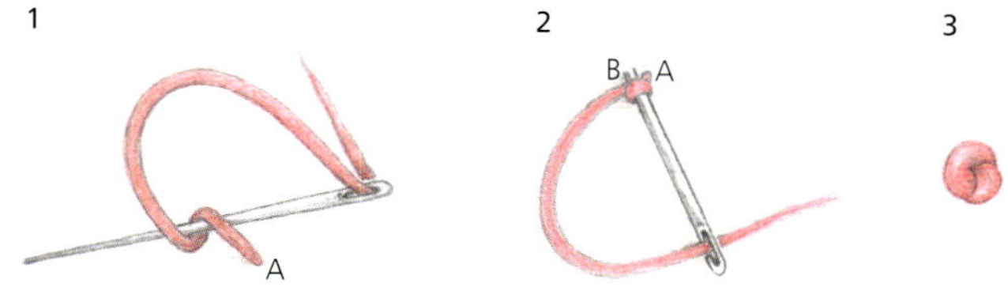

Grab Stitch

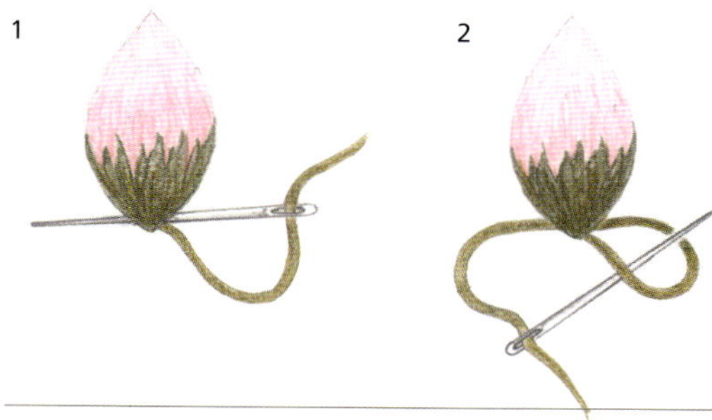

Long and Short Blanket Stitch

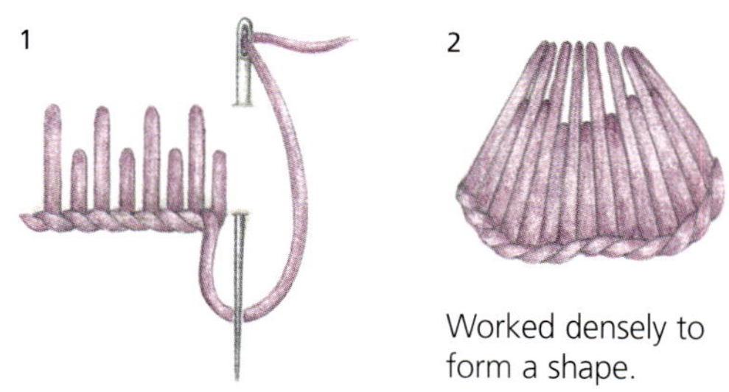

Worked densely to form a shape.

Outline Stitch

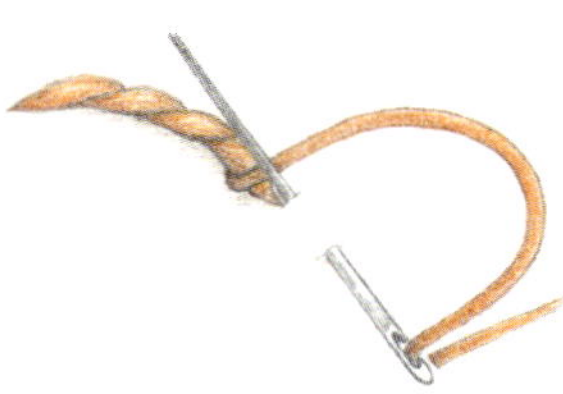

The thread is always kept above the needle.

Padded Satin Stitch

A variety of stitches can be used for the padding, which is then covered with satin stitch.

Pin Stitch

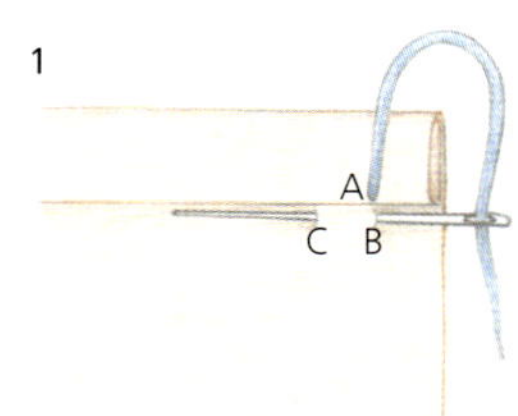

Bring thread out on hem at A. Take needle from B to C on foundation fabric.

Pin Stitch continued...

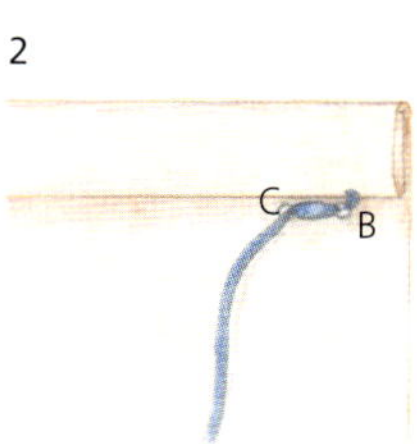

Pull thread through. Take a stitch from B to C. Pull thread tight to form holes.

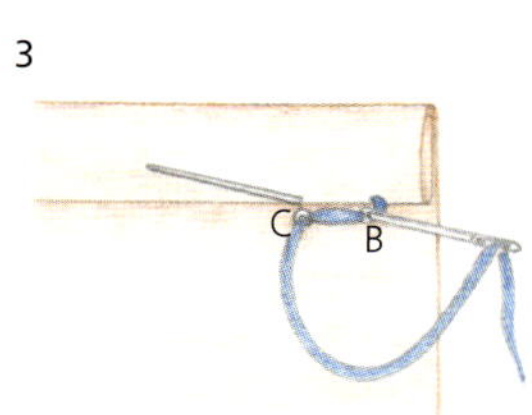

Take needle through hole at B and then through hem immediately above C.

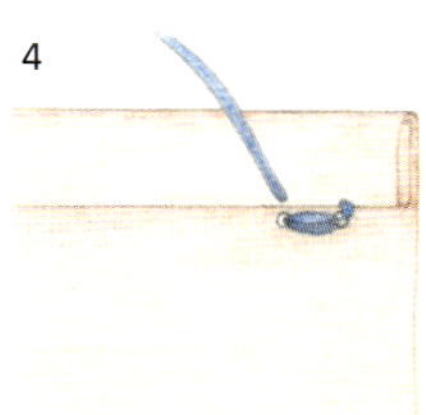

Pull thread through. Continue from step 1.

Pistil Stitch

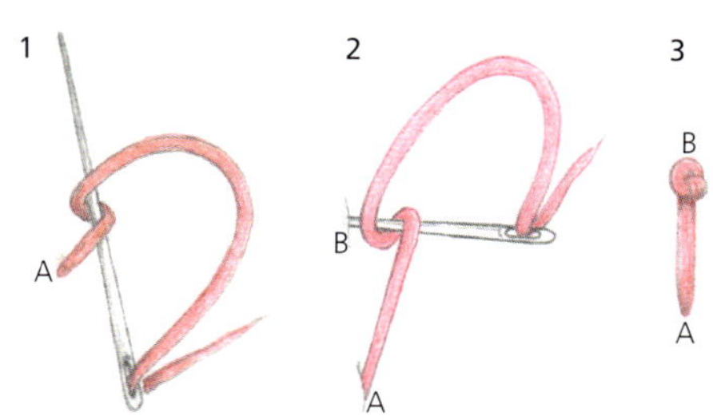

Portuguese Knotted Stem Stitch

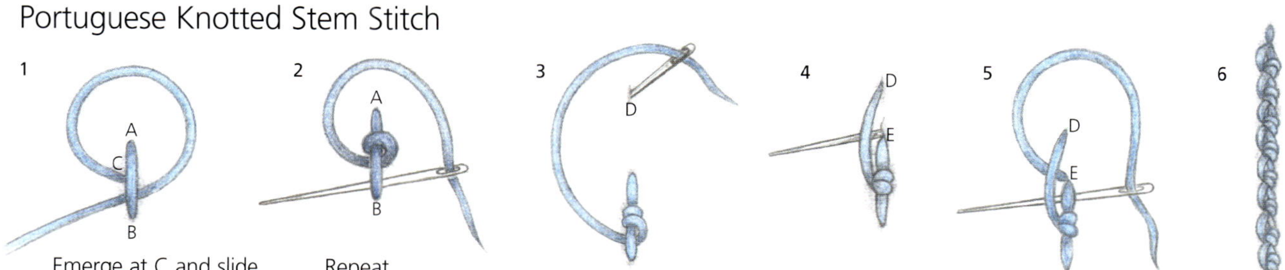

1 Emerge at C and slide needle under AB.

2 Repeat.

Running Stitch

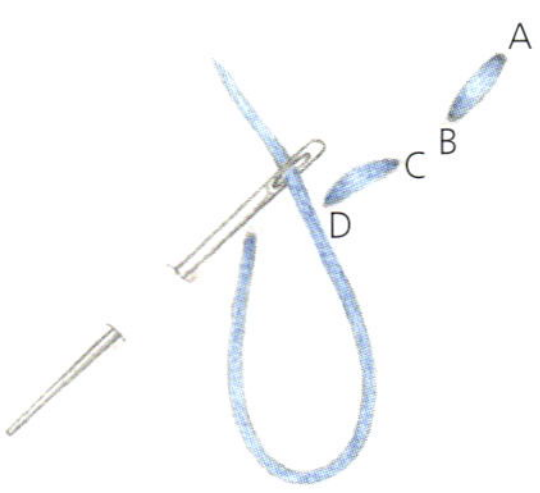

Satin Stitch

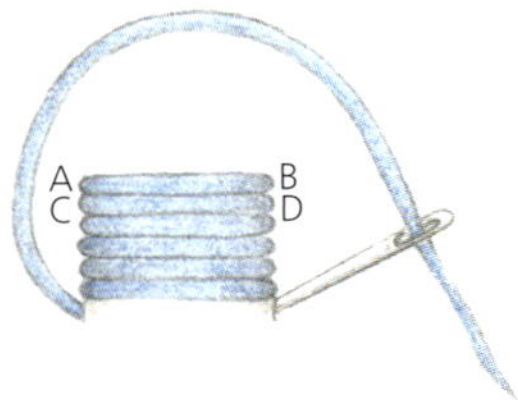

Smocker's Knot

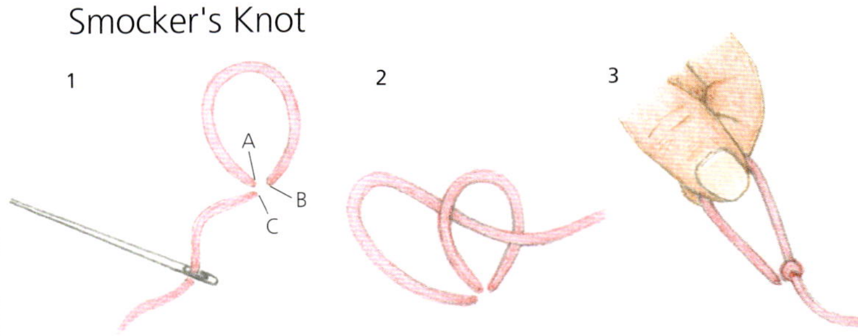

Smocker's Knot continued...

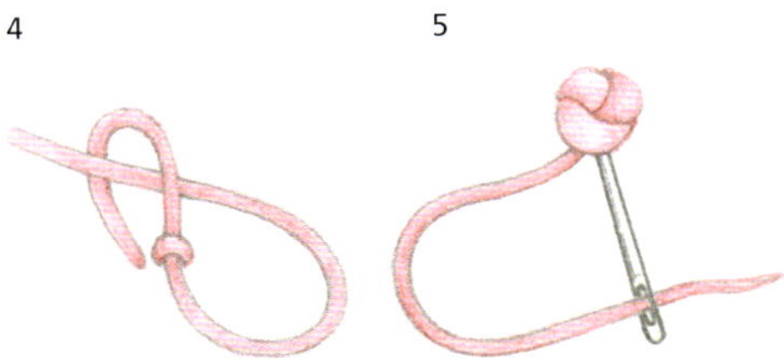

Split Stitch

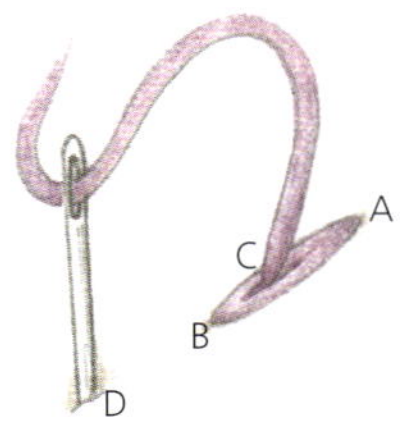

Split Back Stitch

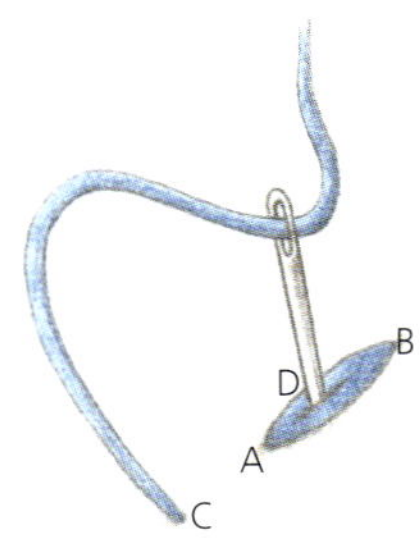

Stem Stitch

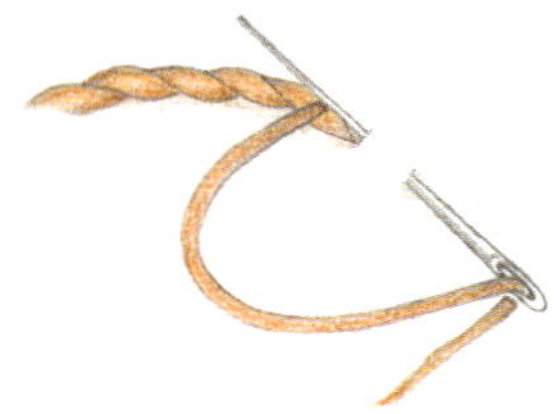

The thread is always kept below the needle.

Trellis Stitch

1

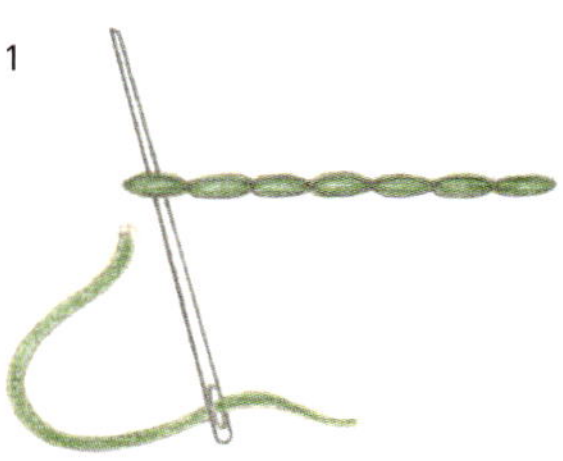

Work a row of back stitch. **Detached stitches** - slide needle under first stitch.

2

Slide needle through loop formed.

3

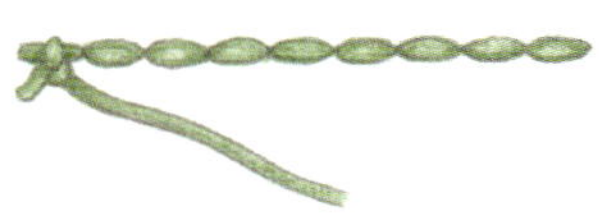

Pull to form a knot.

4

Repeat along the row.

Trellis Stitch continued...

5

Work subsequent rows to and fro.

Twisted Chain Stitch

1

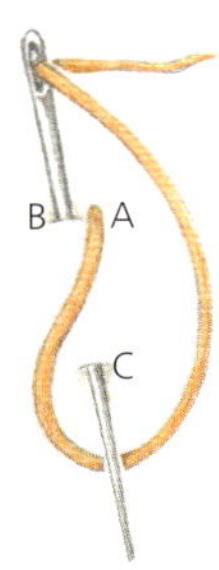

2

End off in the same manner as chain stitch.

Twisted Detached Chain

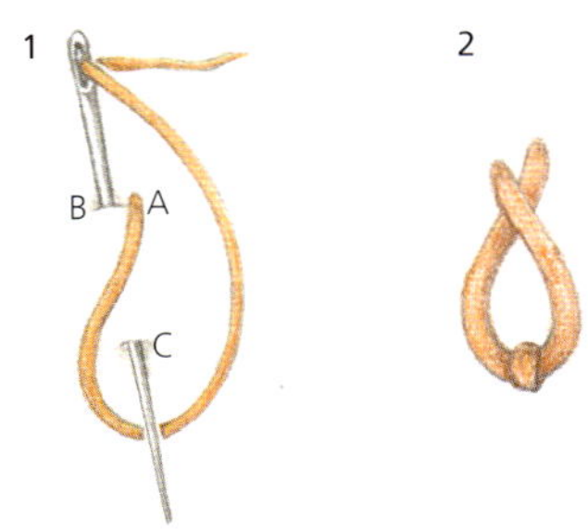

Twisted Ribbon Stitch

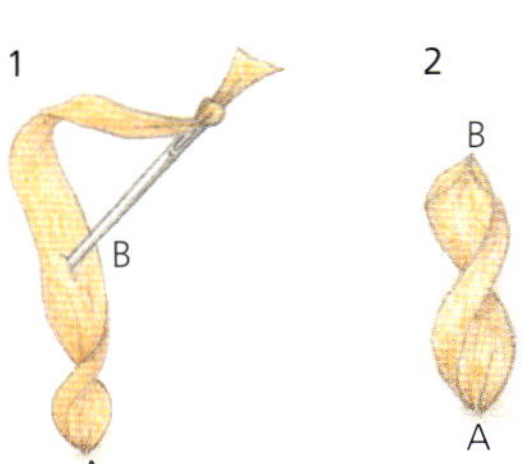

Whipped Reverse Chain

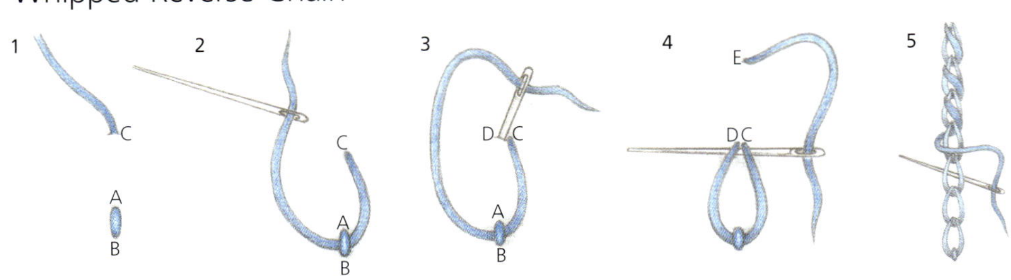

HEAVENLY ROSES

For colour photos and full details, see pages 8 - 17. See the pattern sheet for the scallop template, embroidery designs and lattice diagram.

Preparation for Embroidery

Transferring the design

Transfer the embroidery designs including the placement marks onto the tracing paper using the black pen. Beginning at one corner, place the tracing beneath the fabric, positioning the placement marks 4cm (1 1/2") in from both raw edges. Pin in place. Using a lightbox or window, transfer the design onto the right side of the fabric using the fabric marker *(diag 1)*.

Diag 1

Repeat for the remaining three corners, mirroring the scallop border design as necessary. The rose spray is not mirrored.

Referring to the lattice diagram, rule lines joining the scallop peaks to form a lattice. Using the photograph as a guide for positioning, transfer the scattered buds onto the fabric.

Work the embroidery following the instructions beginning on page 13.

Cutting out

Cream cotton and silk twill

Backing: cut one, 1.4m x 112cm wide (1yd 19" x 44")

Binding: cut seven, each 70cm x 6cm wide (27 1/2" x 2 3/8")

Cutting Layout

Cream cotton and silk twill

1. Backing
2. Binding

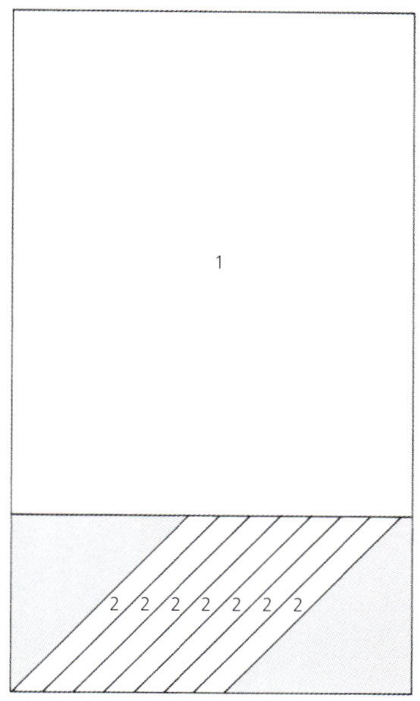

Construction

1. Preparation

Prepare the blanket and attach the backing following steps 1 and 2a of the Construction Method 1 on page 134.

Tack just inside the cutting line around the scalloped edge. Cut away the excess fabric *(diag 2)*.

Diag 2

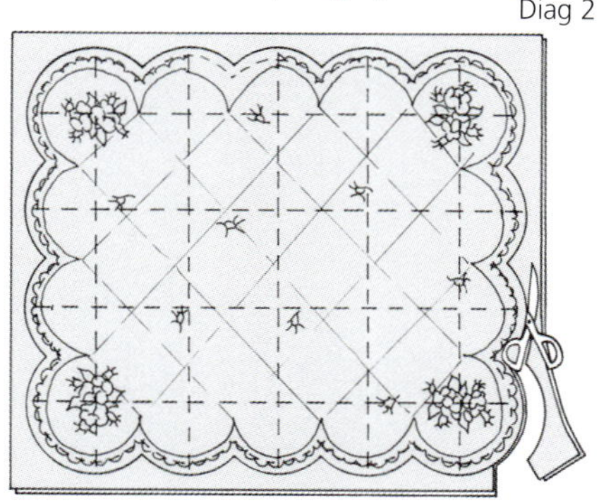

2. Making the binding

With right sides together and matching raw edges, pin and stitch the ends of two binding strips together *(diag 3)*.

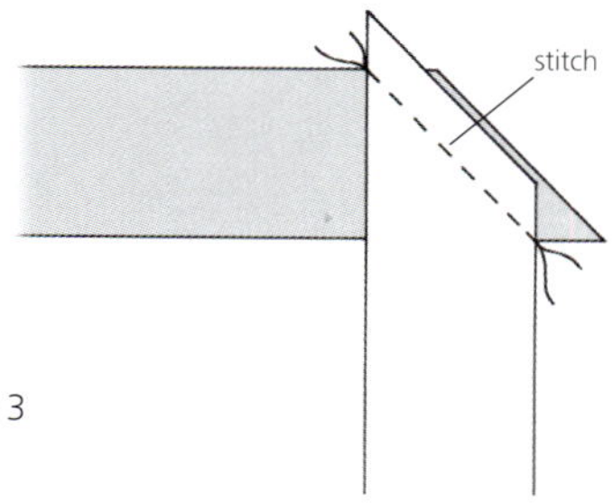

Diag 3

Join all strips in the same manner to form one long strip. Press the seams open. With wrong sides together and matching raw edges, fold the binding in half along the length and press.

3. Attaching the binding

Mark the centre of one scallop with a pin. On the right side of the embroidered blanket, beginning 5cm (2") away from the pin and leaving a 10cm (4") tail extending, start to pin the doubled binding to the scalloped edge matching raw edges *(diag 4)*.

Diag 4

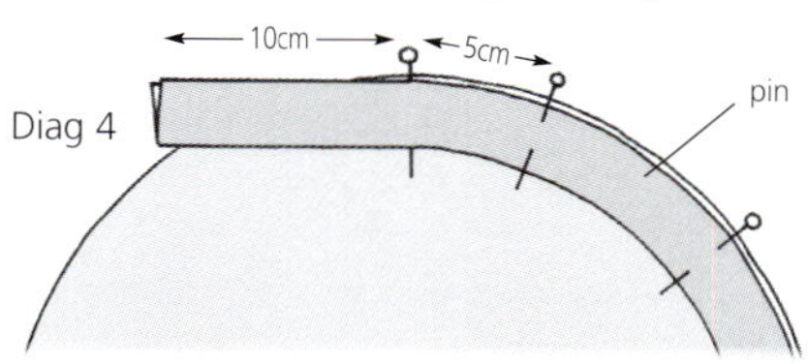

Continue pinning around the edge of the blanket stopping 5cm (2") away from the first pin. Leave a 10cm (4") tail extending and cut away any excess binding *(diag 5)*.

Diag 5

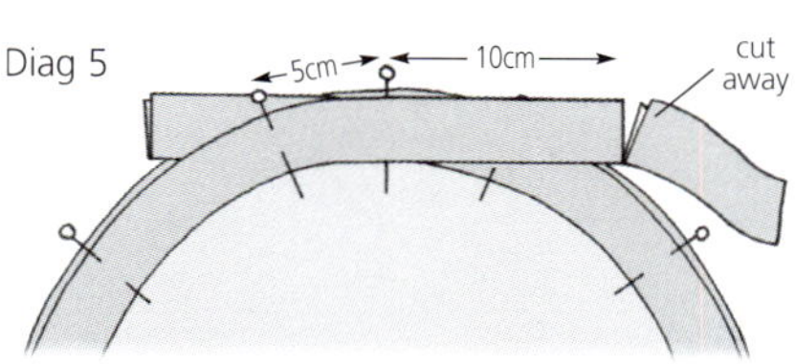

Leaving the tails free and using a 1cm (3/8") seam allowance, stitch the binding in place, pivoting at the point of each scallop *(diag 6)*.

Diag 6

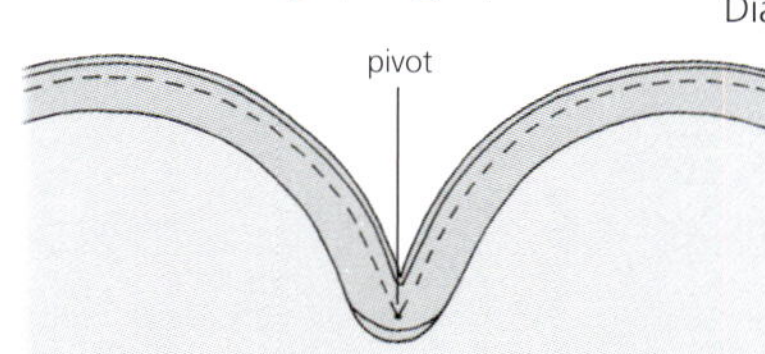

4. Completing the binding

Lay the ends of the binding side by side and mark each with a pin at the centre point of the overlap *(diag 7)*.

Diag 7

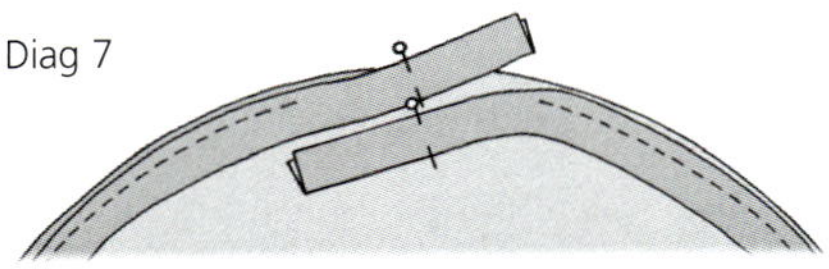

Open out the ends of the bias strips. Cutting along the straight grain (diagonally across the strip), trim the excess lengths of fabric allowing a 1cm (3/8") seam allowance beyond the pin marks *(diag 8)*.

Diag 8

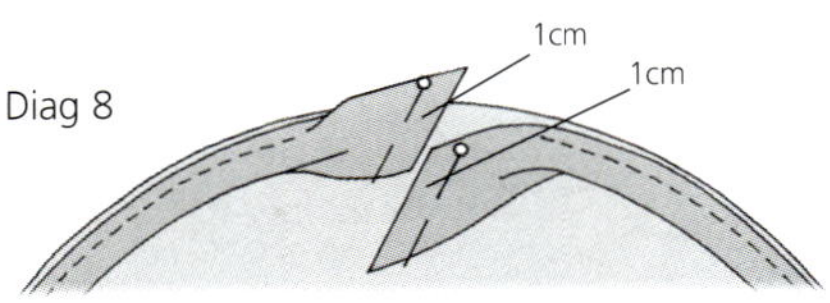

With right sides together, place one end at right angles over the other end. Stitch *(diag 9)*.

Diag 9

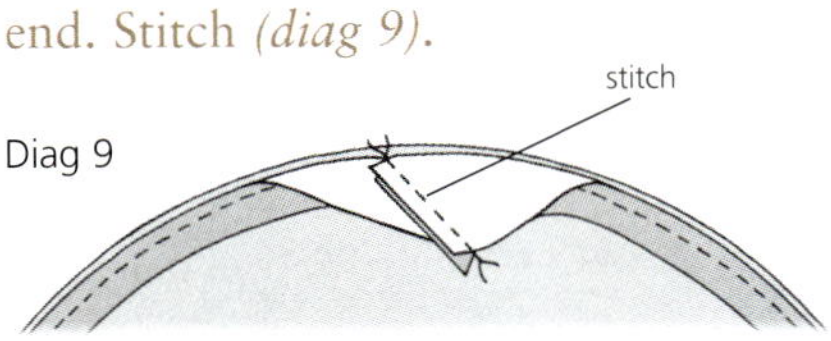

Press the seam open. Refold the binding. Stitch this remaining section of binding to the blanket *(diag 10)*.

Diag 10

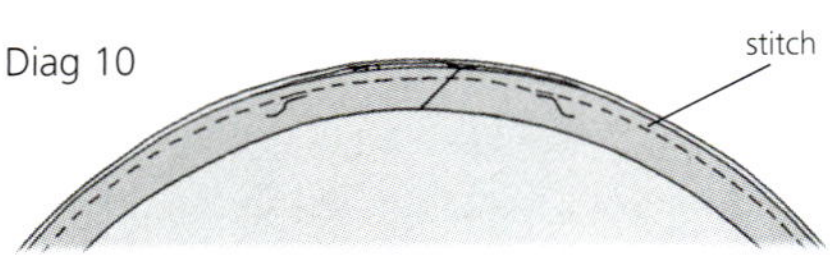

Press the binding towards the outer edge. Fold the binding to the back, enclosing the seam allowance. Pin the binding so the folded edge meets the previous row of stitching. Hand stitch in place along the row of stitching *(diag 11)*.

Diag 11

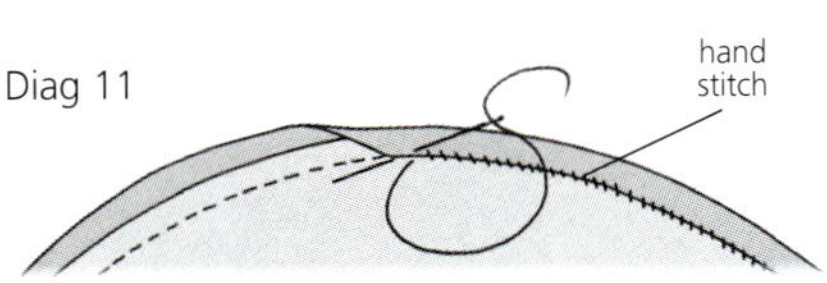

5. Finishing

Remove all tacking threads and gently press the binding.

WINDFLOWER

For colour photos and full details, see pages 18 - 29. See the pattern sheet for the embroidery designs and templates.

Preparation for Embroidery

Preparing the fabric

Following the diagram, measure and work the rows of tacking *(diag 1)*.

Diag 1

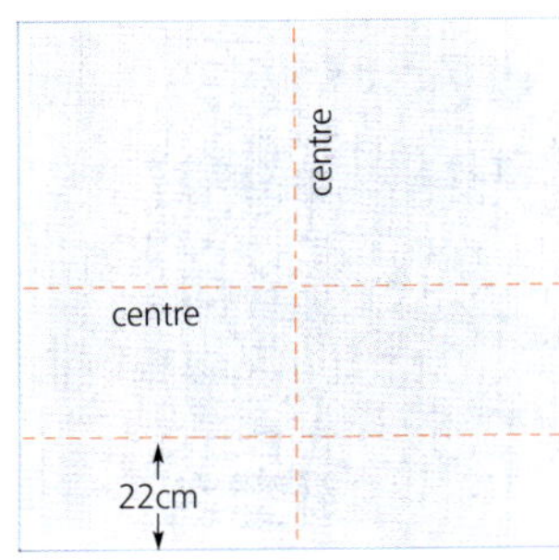

Transfer the design and work the embroidery following the instructions beginning on page 21.

Cutting out

Purple ribbon

Side pieces: cut two, each 83cm (32 5/8") long.

Upper and lower pieces: cut two, each 88cm (34 5/8") long.

Construction

1. Attaching the ribbon

Measure 15cm (6") in from all sides of the blanket and rule lines with the chalk marker *(diag 2)*.

Diag 2

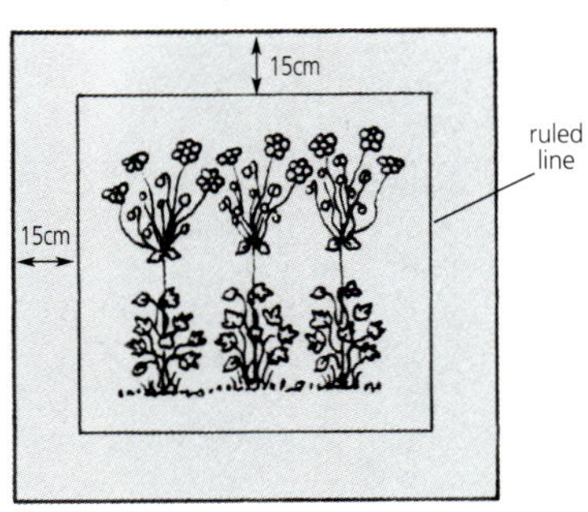

Remove the wire from the edges of the ribbon. With the darker edge facing out, place the two shorter pieces inside the corresponding ruled lines *(diag 3)*.

Diag 3

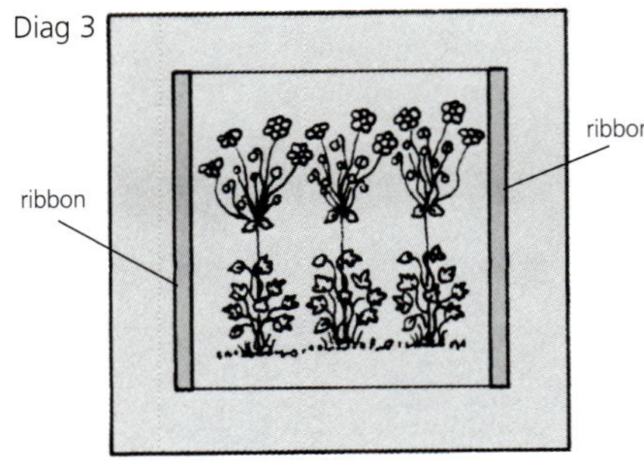

Pin, then machine stitch using thread to match the ribbon. Place the upper and lower pieces inside the remaining ruled lines. Overlap the ends of the attached ribbon *(diag 4)*.

Diag 4

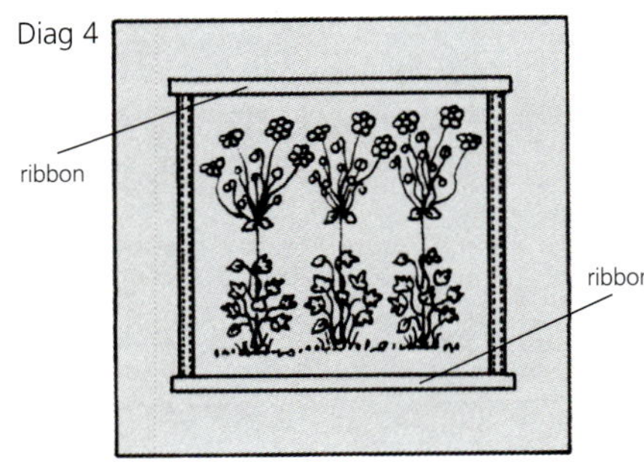

Turn under 1cm (3/8") at the ends *(diag 5)*.

Diag 5

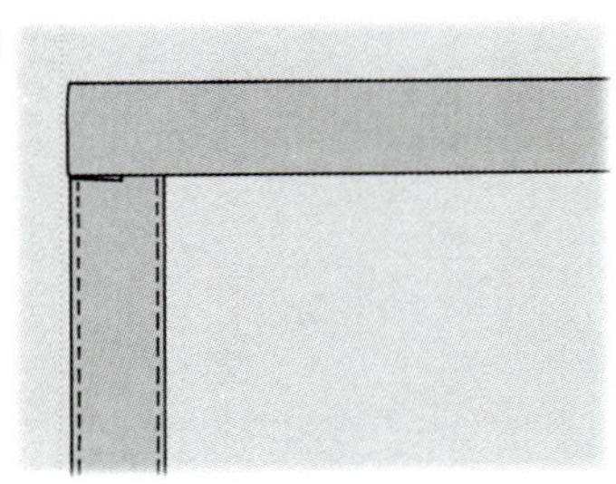

Attach as before. Hand stitch the ends in place *(diag 6)*.

Diag 6

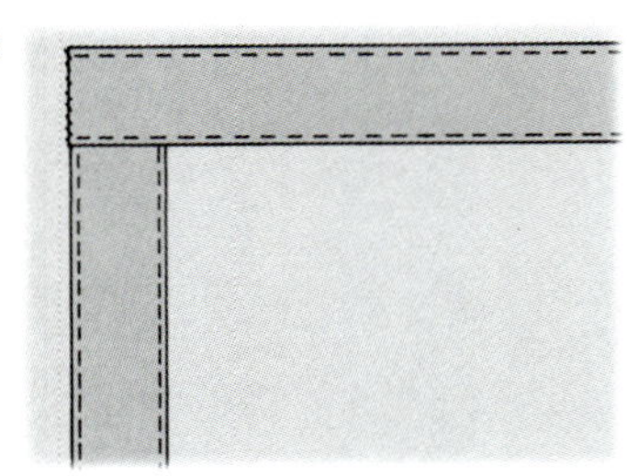

2. Finishing

Complete the blanket following Construction Method 2 on page 139.

Love and Bear Hugs

For colour photos and full details, see pages 30 - 39. See the pattern sheet for the embroidery designs and template.

Cutting out

Hot pink cotton floral print

Dress front: cut one 3.5cm x 10cm wide (1 3/8" x 4")

Band: cut one, 2.5cm x 5cm wide (1" x 2")

Shoulder straps: cut two, each 3cm x 2.5cm wide (1 1/4" x 1")

Cutting layouts

Hot pink cotton floral print

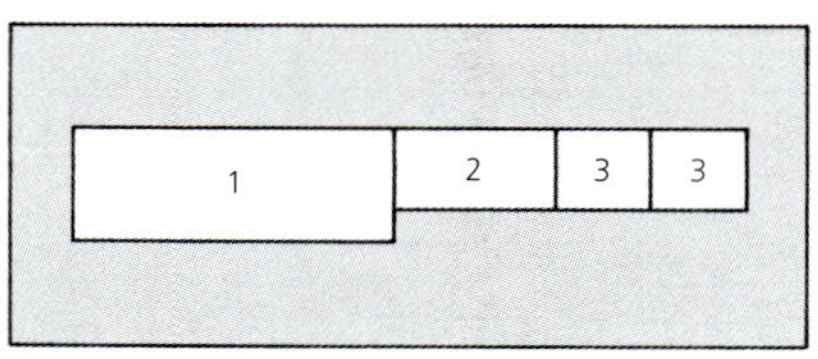

1. Sundress front
2. Band
3. Strap

Making the sundress

1. Front

Fold under 5mm (3/16") on one long edge of the front and press. Pin the folded edge to the heading on the lace edging for the hem. Stitch close to the folded edge *(diag 1).*

Diag 1

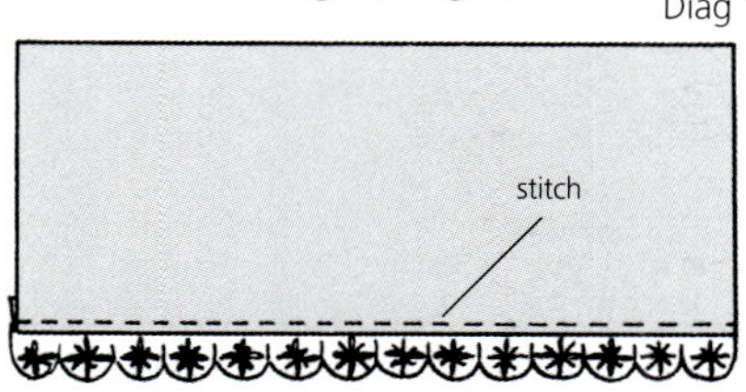

Stitch two rows of machine gathering across the upper edge of the front.

2. Band

With the right side of the band facing the wrong side of the front, pull up and pin the gathered edge of the front to fit the band *(diag 2).*

Diag 2

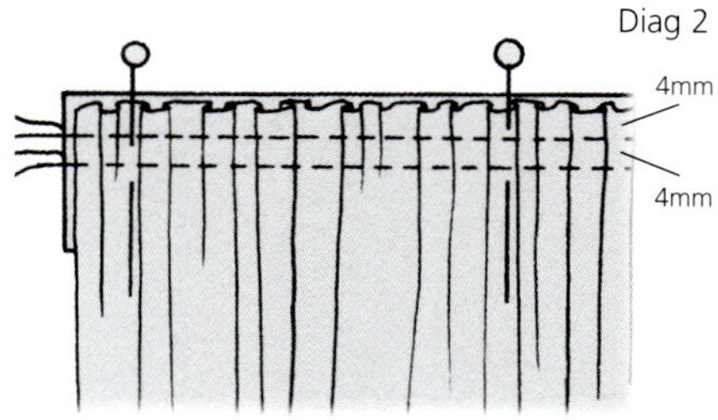

Stitch between the rows of gathering.

Turn under 6mm (1/4") on the remaining long edge of the band and press. Fold the band over to the front and pin, just covering the previous stitch line. Stitch close to the folded edge *(diag 3).*

Diag 3

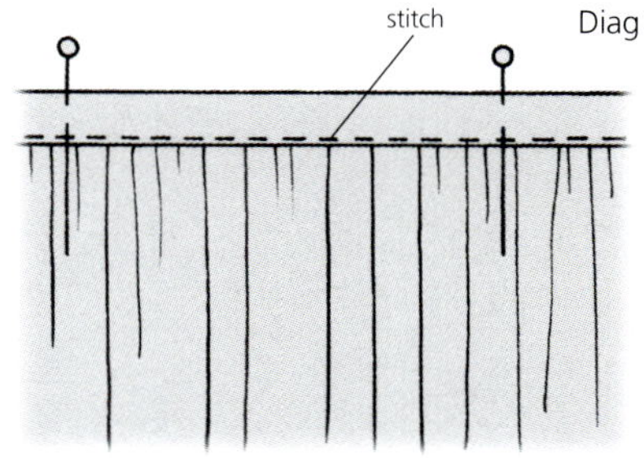

Turn under 6mm (1/4") on each side of the sundress and press.

3. Straps

Fold under 6mm (1/4") on both long sides of each strap and press. Fold in half lengthwise and press. Stitch close to the folded edges *(diag 4).*

Diag 4

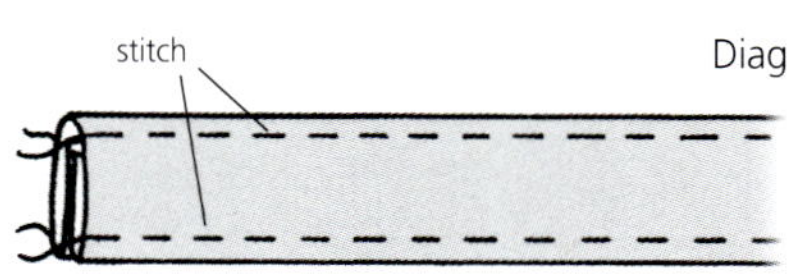

Embroidery

Make the bear and attach the sundress and ribbon following the step-by-step instructions on page 38. When complete, work the remaining embroidery.

Construction

Complete the blanket following Construction Method 1 on pages 137 - 139.

Lullaby

For colour photos and full details, see pages 40 - 49. See the pattern sheet for the embroidery designs and templates.

Preparation for Embroidery

Preparing the flannel

Following the diagram, measure and work the rows of tacking using pale machine sewing thread *(diag 1).*

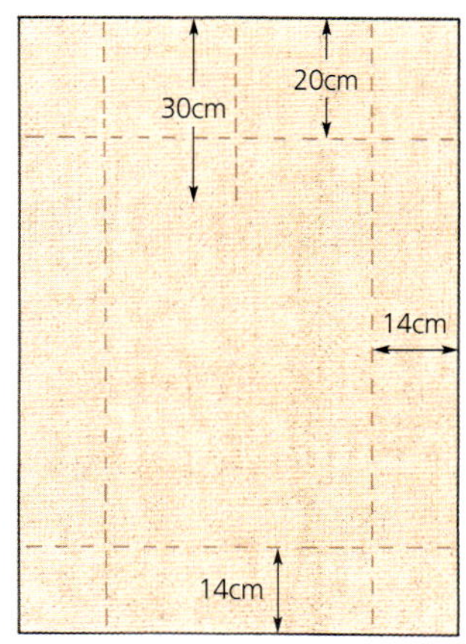

Diag 1

Transfer the design and work the embroidery following the instructions beginning on page 45.

Construction

1. Preparation

Prepare the blanket following step 1 of Construction Method 1 on page 134.

Trace the upper edge template onto paper and cut out. Matching placement marks, position the template onto the right side of the fabric at the upper left corner. Transfer the shaping to the embroidered blanket. Flip the tracing and repeat for the upper right corner. Transfer the corner template to the lower corners in the same manner *(diag 2).* Cut out the blanket around the shape.

2. Attaching the wadding

Lay the wadding on a flat surface. With the right side facing up, place the blanket over the wadding. Pin the layers together ensuring they are smooth. Working outwards from the centre, tack the layers together in a grid. Tack around the four sides 1cm (3/8") in from the raw edges of the blanket *(diag 3)*. Trim the wadding to match the blanket.

Diag 2

Diag 3

3. Attaching the piping

Mark the centre point of the upper edge with a pin. With right sides together and matching raw edges, pin the piping to the blanket beginning at the centre of the upper edge. Leave a 1cm (3/8") tail extending past the centre point stitching line.

When pinning around the curves, clip the piping heading at 1cm (3/8") intervals *(diag 4)*.

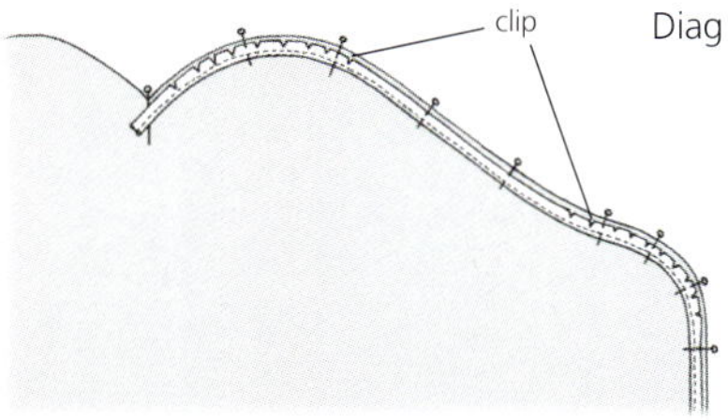

Diag 4

Continue until reaching the beginning. Trim any excess length of piping allowing a 1cm (3/8") tail to overlap *(diag 5)*.

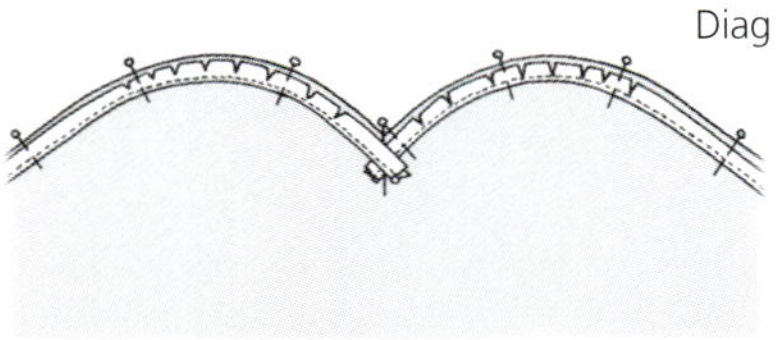

Diag 5

To reduce bulk, unpick the stitching on the overlapping ends and trim the cords level with the marked centre point *(diag 6)*. Re-pin the piping overlapping the ends.

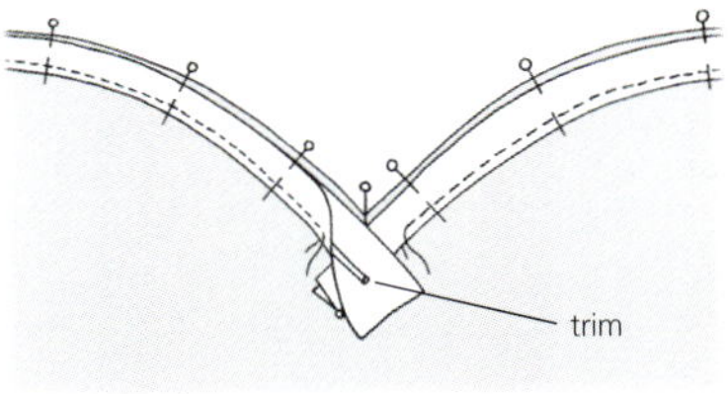

Diag 6

Stitch around the blanket along the piping stitch line. Begin at the exact centre point of the peak and hold the other tail out of the way *(diag 7)*.

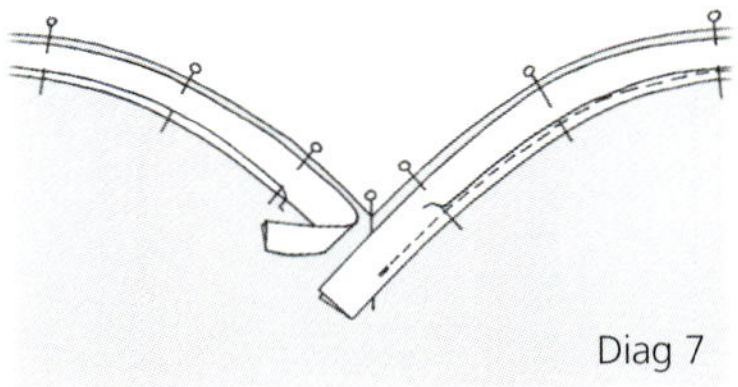

Diag 7

Complete in the same manner. The two tails will remain separate *(diag 8)*. Snip the blanket seam allowance at the marked centre point almost to the stitch line.

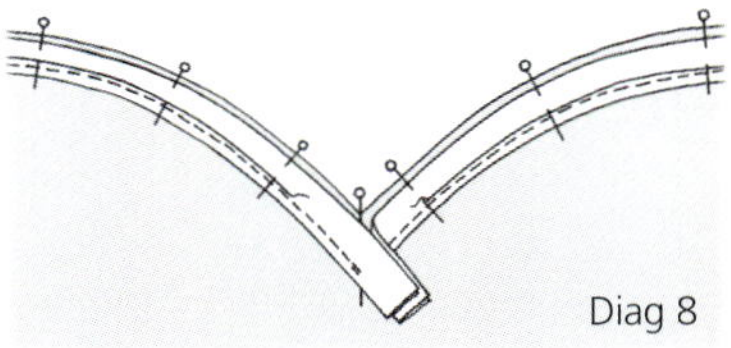

Diag 8

4. Attaching the backing

Lay the backing fabric right side up on a flat surface. With right sides together, centre the blanket on the backing. The piping is sandwiched between. Pin and tack the layers together in the same manner as for the wadding. Trim the backing to match the front. Stitch the layers together, stitching between the previous stitching and the corded edge of the piping. Begin at the centre point of the peak as before, keeping the piping tails out of the way. Do not stitch across the centre point *(diag 9)*. Leave a 20cm (8") opening at the centre of the lower edge.

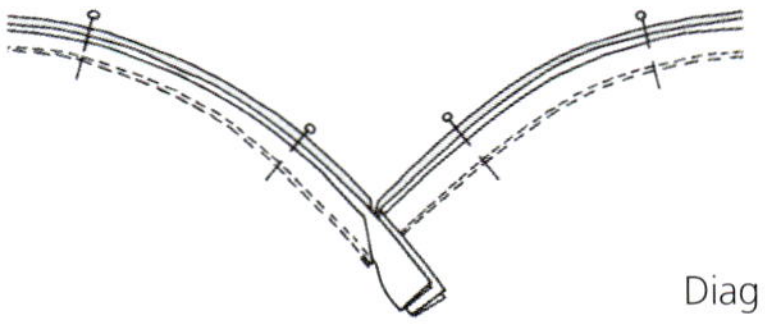

Diag 9

Clip the curves. Remove the tacking and turn the blanket to the right side through the opening. Hand stitch the opening closed and press.

The Duckling

For colour photos and full details, see pages 50 - 57. See the pattern sheet for the embroidery design and templates.

Preparation for Embroidery

Blanketing

Following the diagram, measure and work the rows of tacking using pale machine sewing thread *(diag 1)*.

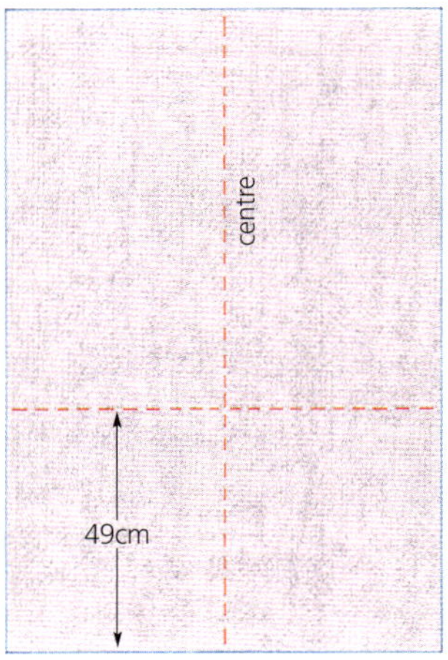

Diag 1

Homespun

Using the templates, cut out two pieces for the beak and two pieces for each foot.

Transfer the design and work the embroidery following the instructions beginning on page 53.

Construction

Complete the blanket following Construction Method 1 on pages 137 - 139.

Fantasia

For colour photos and full details, see pages 58 - 71. See the pattern sheet for the embroidery designs.

Preparation for Embroidery

Preparing the fabric

Following the diagram, measure and work the rows of tacking using pale machine sewing thread. Mark the dots with the pencil. X marks the centre of the appliqué *(diag 1).*

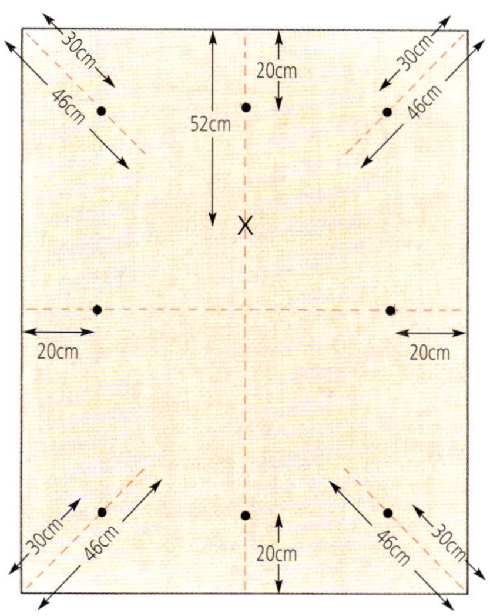

Diag 1

Transfer the design and work the embroidery following the instructions beginning on page 61.

Cutting out

Cream duchess satin

Side binding: cut two, each 152cm x 14cm wide (60" x 5 1/2")

Upper and lower binding: cut two, each 122cm x 14cm wide (48" x 5 1/2")

Cutting layout

Cream duchess satin

1. Side binding
2. Upper and lower binding

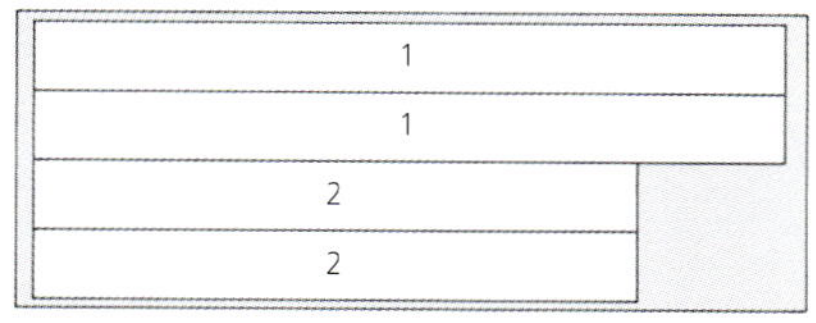

Construction

Complete the blanket following Construction Method 2 on page 139.

Wood Spirits

For colour photos and full details, see pages 72 - 81. See the pattern sheet for the embroidery design, stitch direction diagram and templates.

Construction

Complete the blanket following Construction Method 1 on pages 137 - 139.

Posies

For colour photos and full details, see pages 82 - 89. See the pattern sheet for the embroidery designs and placement diagram.

Preparation for Embroidery

Preparing the fabric

Following the diagram, measure and work the rows of tacking using pale machine sewing thread. Begin with the centre rows of tacking *(diag 1).*

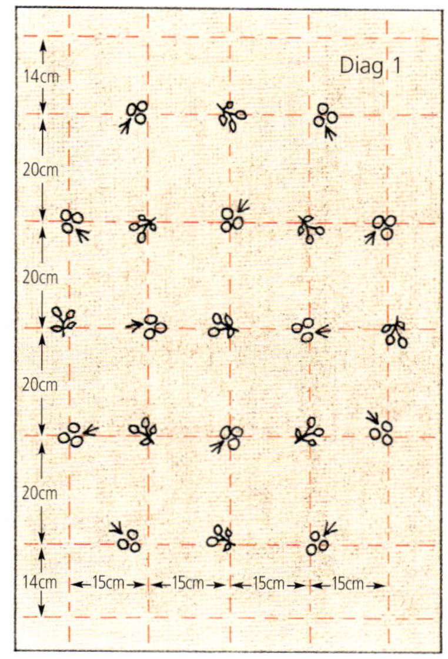

Transfer the design and work the embroidery following the instructions beginning on page 85.

Construction

Complete the blanket following Construction Method 1 on pages 137 - 139.

Hedgerow Flowers

For colour photos and full details, see pages 90 - 107. See the pattern sheet for the embroidery designs, templates, patterns and needlepoint charts.

Cutting out

Where pattern pieces are not provided, cut the pieces according to the measurements on the next page.

Cream homespun

Base for flowers in basket: cut one, 15cm (6") square

Blue chambray

Skirt: cut one, 12cm x 15.5cm wide (4 3/4" x 6 1/8")

White organdy

Apron: cut one, 12cm x 14cm wide (4 3/4" x 5 1/2")

Apron waistband: cut one, 2.5cm x 5.5cm wide (1" x 2 1/4")

Cutting layout

Cream homespun

1. Body 2. Arm

3. Base for flowers in basket

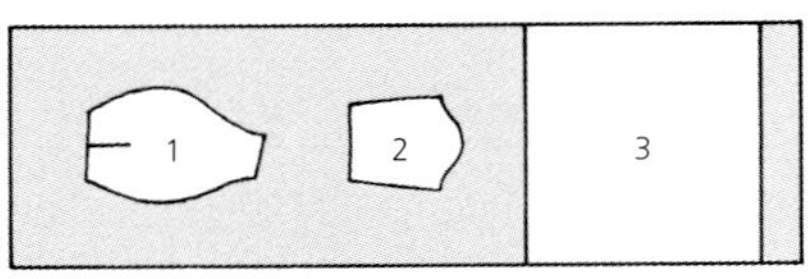

Blue chambray

4. Bodice 5. Skirt 6. Sleeve

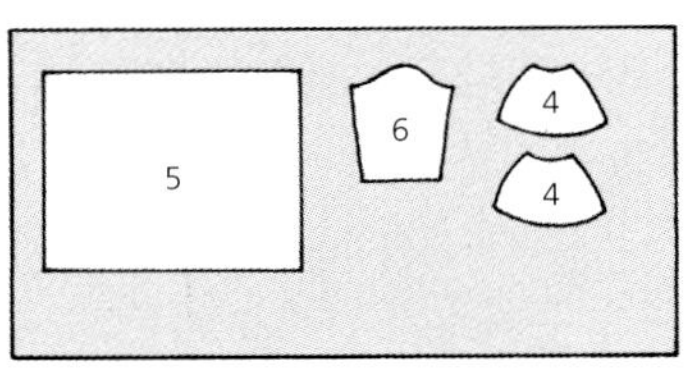

White organdy

7. Apron 8. Apron waistband

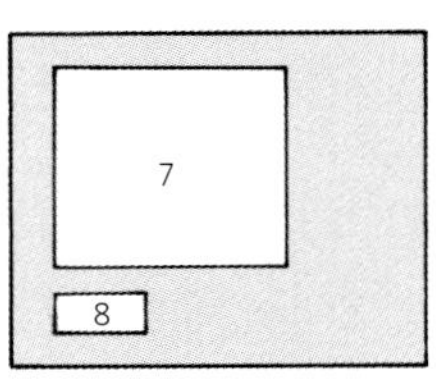

Making the rabbit

All seam allowances are 5mm (3/16") unless otherwise specified.

1. Attaching the body

Hand stitch the body to the blanket, leaving a small opening in the back as indicated on the pattern. Fill the body with a small amount of fibre-fill *(diag 1)*. Stitch the opening closed.

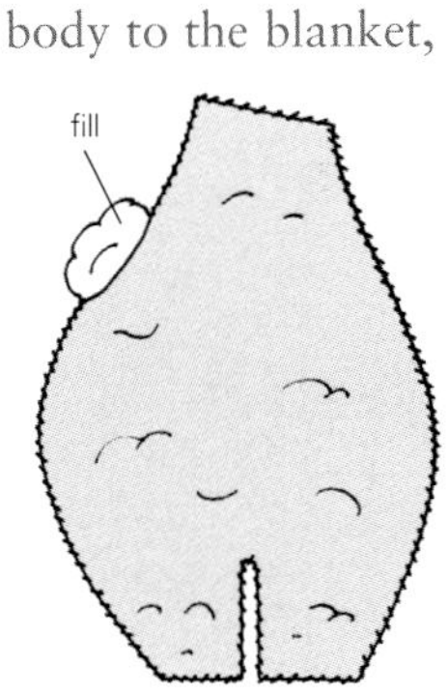

Diag 1

2. Making the bloomers

Attach the wider lace edging to one long edge of the white batiste by rolling and whipping the seam *(diag 2)*.

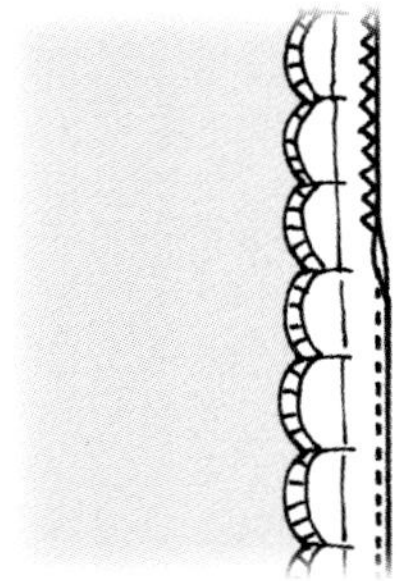

Diag 2

At the centre of this edge draw a 3.5 cm (1 3/8") long vertical line with the fabric marker. Machine stitch 5mm (3/16") on each side of the line. Cut along the line and clip into the corners *(diag 3)*.

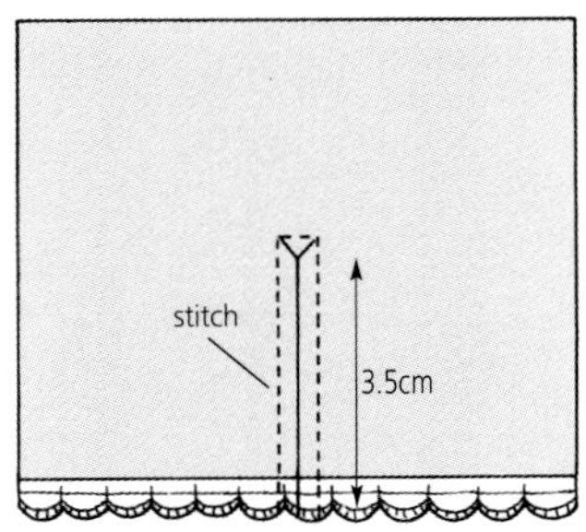

Diag 3

Turn under and press. Turn under 5mm (3/16") on the two outer edges and press.

Using AZ, anchor a thread on each side of each leg, 5mm (3/16") up from the lace edge seam line. Work running stitches into the centre of each ankle, leaving all four threads dangling *(diag 4)*.

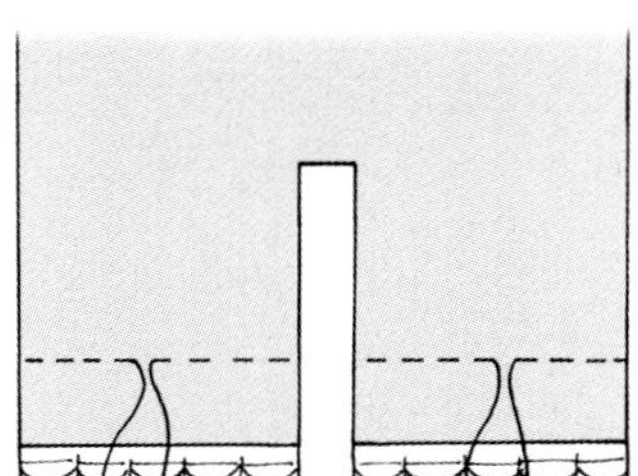

Diag 4

Turn under 5mm (3/16") at the waist and work a row of gathering stitches.

Pin the bloomers in position over the body. Hand stitch along the inner and outer leg edges.

Pull up the waist gathering thread to fit and secure. Pull up the gathering threads for the ankles and tie in a bow with a double knot *(diag 5)*.

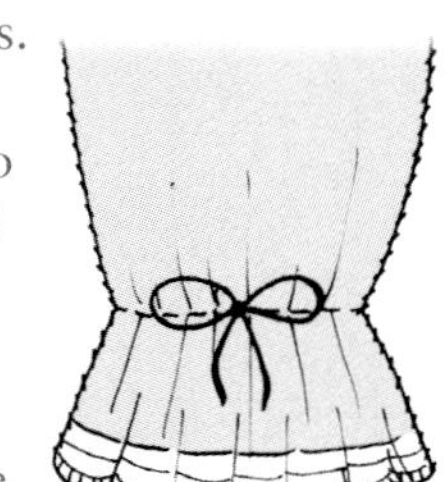

Diag 5

3. Making the arm

Fold under the seam allowance at the wrist edge of the homespun and run a gathering thread along the edge.

With right sides together, machine stitch the under arm seam. Turn through to the right side.

Gather the top of the arm *(diag 6)*.

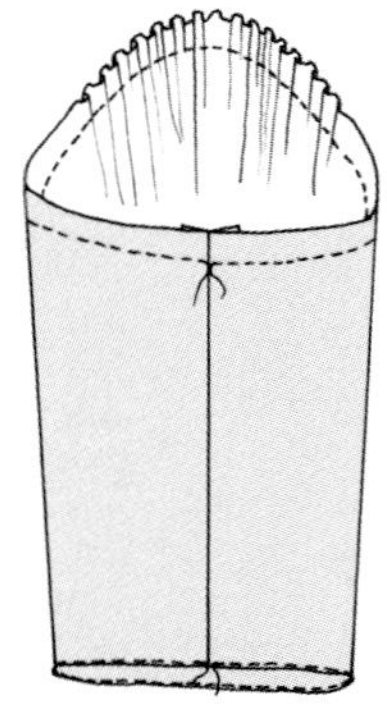

Diag 6

Insert the embroidered paw into the wrist. Pull up the thread to fit and secure. Hand stitch *(diag 7)*.

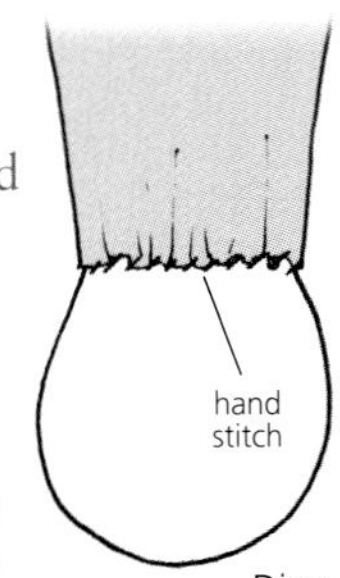

Diag 7

Insert a 4.5cm (1 3/4") length of pipe cleaner into the arm, then fill the arm with fibre-fill. Pull up the gathering thread and secure *(diag 8)*.

Diag 8

4. Making the sleeve

On the blue chambray, turn under 3mm (1/8") at the wrist edge. Gather the wrist edge and attach the narrow lace edging with small hand stitches *(diag 9)*.

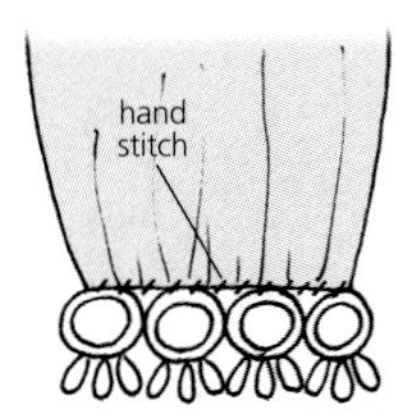

Diag 9

With right sides together, machine stitch the under arm seam. Turn to the right side.

Gather the upper edge of the sleeve. Insert the arm and pull up the gathering thread to fit. Turn the seam allowance in and hand stitch.

5. Forming the bodice

With right sides facing, stitch the bodice pieces together, leaving the lower edge open. Turn to the right side and press. Using small hand stitches, attach a piece of narrow lace edging to the neck edge *(diag 10)*.

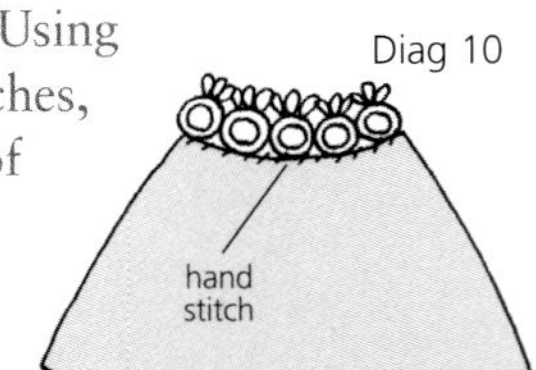

Diag 10

6. Forming the skirt

Starting 1cm (3/8") from one short side and finishing the same distance from the other side, draw vertical parallel lines at 5mm (3/16") intervals with the fabric marker.

Referring to the photographs and using AZ, embroider alternate rows of stem stitch and coral stitch.

Remove all traces of the fabric marker. Place face down on a well padded surface and press.

Turn up a small double hem, hand stitch and press.

Turn under 5mm (3/16") on each side and press.

Gather the waist 5mm (3/16") from the raw edge, to match the bodice.

With right sides together and raw edges even, stitch the bodice to the gathered edge of the skirt *(diag 11)*. Press the seam towards the bodice.

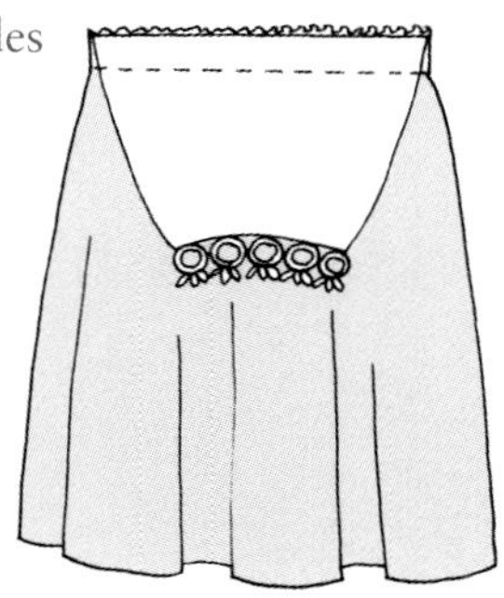

Diag 11

7. Making the apron

With wrong sides together, fold up 4cm (1 1/2") on the lower edge and press. Press two more fold lines 7mm (5/16") apart above the first. Using BZ, form the pintucks by working tiny running stitches close to the fold lines. Press the tucks towards the lower edge *(diag 12)*.

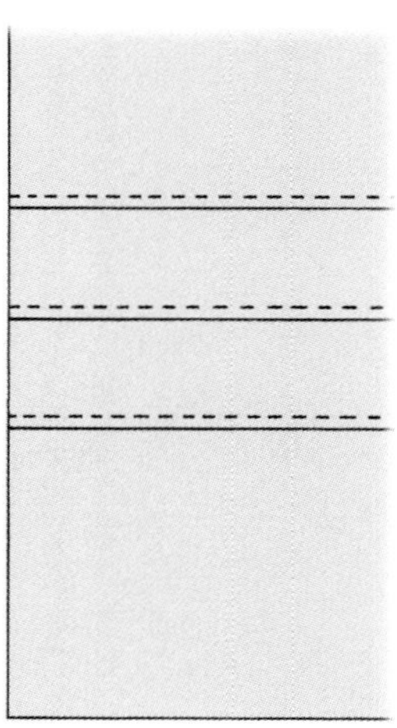

Diag 12

On the left edge, fold under a 7mm (5/16") double hem. Pin stitch the hem by hand, using the no. 28 tapestry needle and BZ *(diag 13)*.

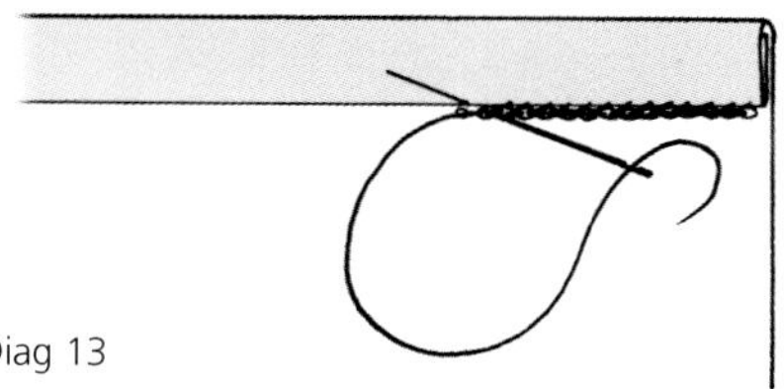

Diag 13

At the lower edge, turn under a 12mm (1/2") double hem and pin stitch in the same manner as before.

Gather the waist, pull up to measure 5cm (2") and secure.

Fold the waistband in half along the length and press. Open out the band. Fold in each long edge to meet the centre fold line and press *(diag 14)*.

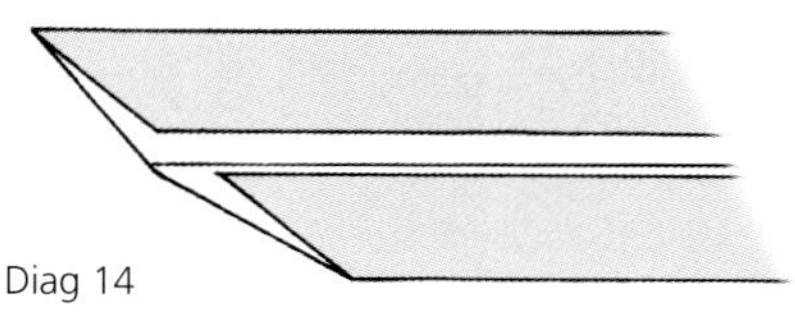

Diag 14

Fold in 5mm (3/16") on the left short end. Place the waist edge of the apron into the waist band, aligning the upper edge with the centre pressed line *(diag 15)*.

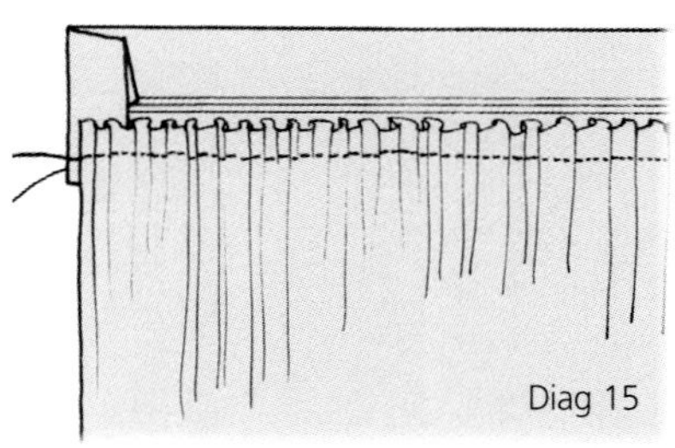

Diag 15

Fold the band over the raw edge. Tack and pin stitch *(diag 16)*.

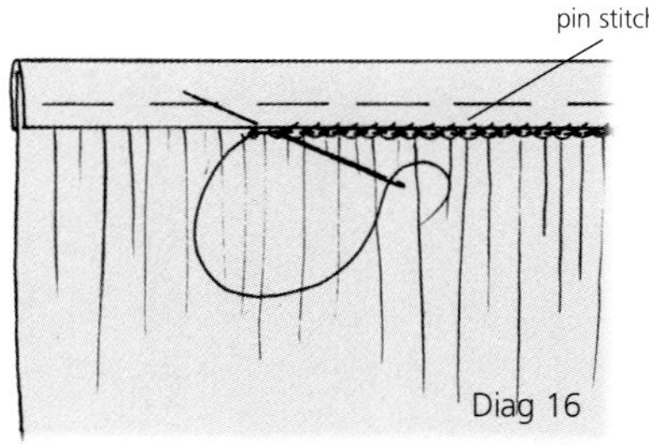

Diag 16

Fold under 5mm (3/16") on the right edge of the apron and press.

Tuck this edge around the edge of the skirt *(diag 17)*. Tack through both layers.

Diag 17

8. Attaching the arm

Bend the arm into a slight curve. Place the arm onto the bodice at the marked position. Arranging the gathers on the sleeve head and using invisible stitches, firmly secure the arm to the bodice *(diag 18)*.

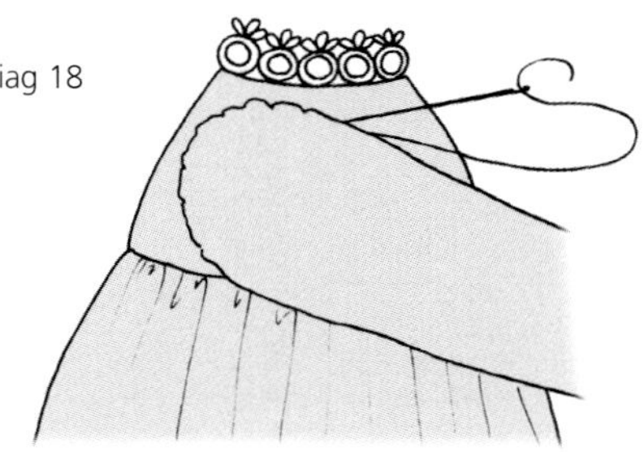

Diag 18

9. Attaching the clothes

Place the dress and apron over the rabbit at the marked position. Pin and hand stitch, leaving the hem free.

10. Finishing the basket

Attach the basket of flowers over the rabbit's arm, catching the paw down.

11. Making the apron bow

Using the fabric marker, mark the white satin ribbon as shown *(diag 19)*. Secure a thread at the first mark. Take a tiny running stitch at each mark. Pull up to create eight loops and two tails. Secure into position at the left end of the waistband.

12. Constructing the blanket

Complete the blanket following Construction Method 2 on page 139.

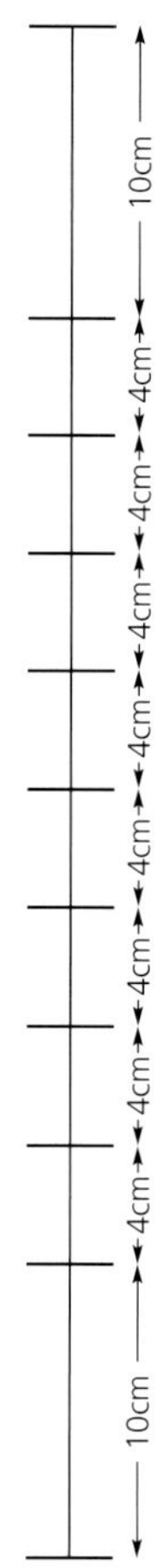

Diag 19

ANGELS DREAMING

For colour photos and full details, see pages 108 - 113. See the pattern sheet for the embroidery designs.

Preparation for Embroidery

Borders

The two blue stem stitch borders are not marked onto the fabric; the starting points are found by measuring from the outer edge and the rows of stem stitch are then worked following the weave in the fabric. Beginning at one corner, measure in 10cm (4") from both edges and mark with pins. Measure in 19cm (7 1/2") from both edges and mark with pins *(diag 1)*.

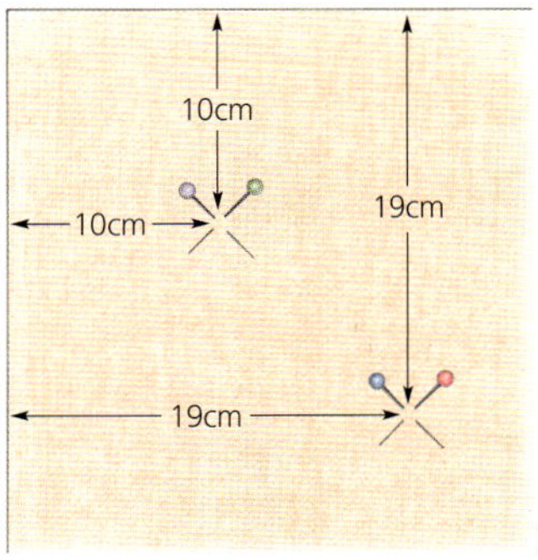

Diag 1

Repeat for the remaining three corners. Work the borders following the embroidery instructions before transferring the designs.

Transfer the designs and work the remaining embroidery following the instructions beginning on page 111.

Construction

Refer to Construction Method 1 on pages 137 - 139, omitting Step 4 (Attaching the piping).

After Step 5 (Finishing) complete the binding by stitching a second row of top stitching 8mm (5/16") away from the first.

THE PIGLET

For colour photos and full details, see pages 114 - 123. See the pattern sheet for the embroidery designs and stitch direction diagrams.

Cutting out - Bag

Check fabric

Outer bag: cut one, 60cm x 62cm wide (23 1/2" x 24 3/8")

Base: cut one circle, 21cm (8 1/4") in diameter

Straps: cut two, each 57cm x 6cm wide (22 3/8" x 2 3/8")

Lining

Inner bag: cut one, 51cm x 62cm wide (20" x 24 3/8")

Base: cut one circle, 21cm (8 1/4") in diameter

Cutting layouts

Check fabric

1. Outer bag 2. Base 3. Strap

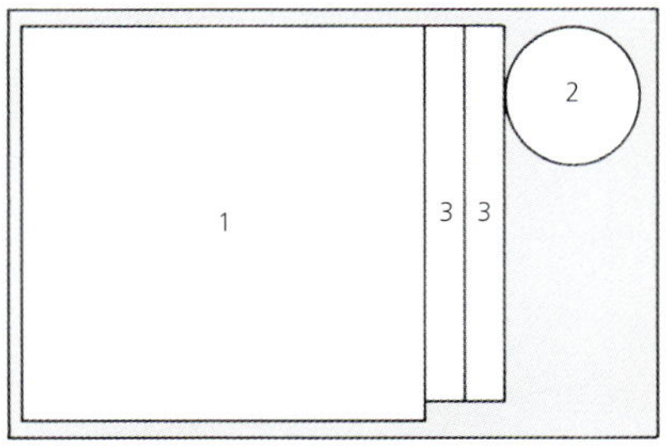

Lining

4. Inner bag 2. Base

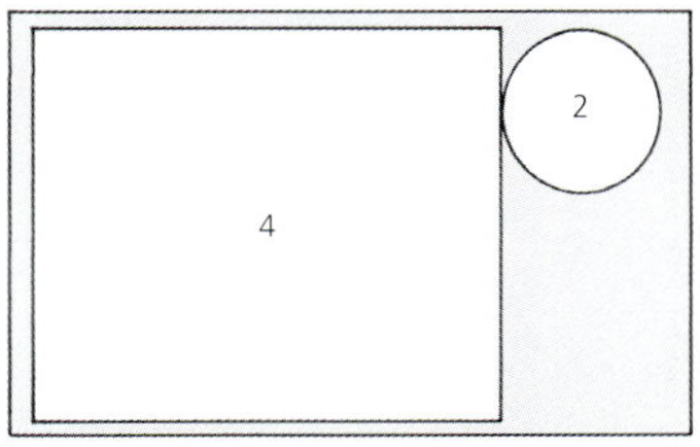

Cutting out - Blanket

The requirements for the framed effect on the blanket will depend on your choice of fabrics. Refer to the following instructions for details on calculating fabric.

An interesting and effective border can be achieved by combining both plain and check fabrics.

As a mitre (or diagonal join) occurs at each corner of the border, it is important to accurately match the fabric so that, when joined, a whole square or pattern is retained at the corner.

The dimensions of the pieces need to be determined according to the size and colour distribution of the checks.

Our blanket uses a large check with a repeating colour sequence, but the following method can be adapted to suit most fabrics with a repeating pattern that requires matching at the corners.

Calculating the border measurements

Check fabric

Cut two strips the desired width plus seam allowances and as long as the sides of the blanketing, allowing several extra checks in order to match the corners.

Cut two more strips in a similar manner using the length of the upper and lower ends of the blanketing.

Place the blanketing on a flat surface. With the ends overlapping, lay the four check strips evenly around the blanketing, forming a rectangular frame *(diag 1)*.

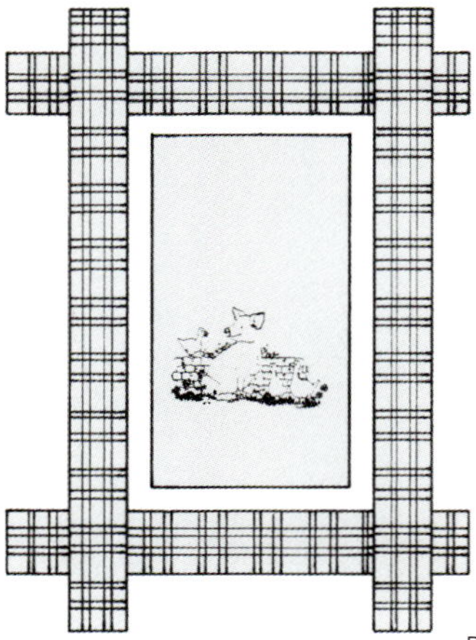

Diag 1

Manipulate the strips to achieve a matched check at each corner and pin. Trim away the excess fabric *(diag 2)*.

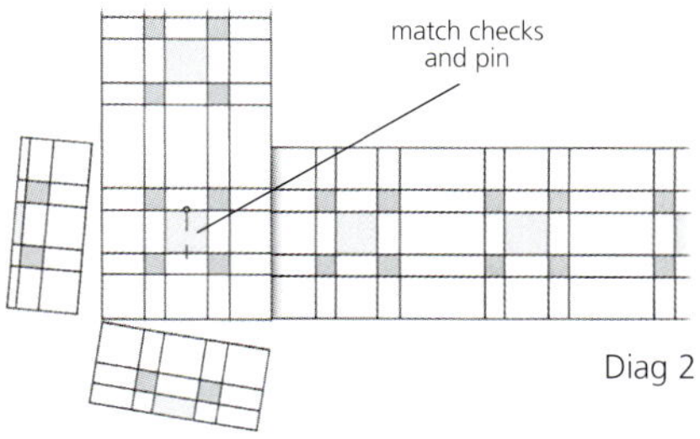

Diag 2

Plain fabric

Ensuring the blanketing is centred, measure the distance between the raw edges of the blanketing and the check frame *(diag 3)*.

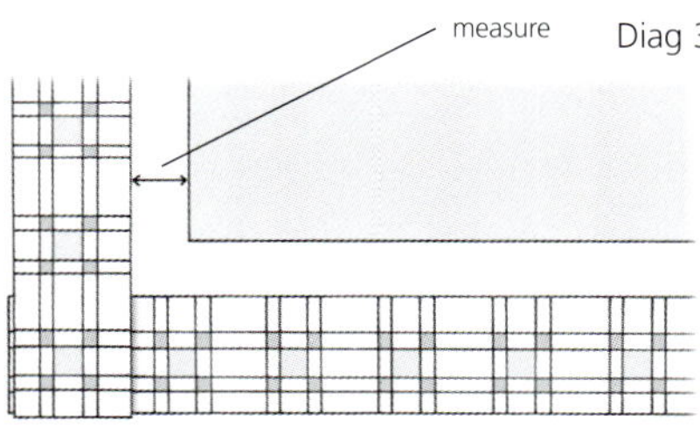

Diag 3

Add 2cm (3/4") to this measurement for the seam allowances. This new measurement will be the cut width of the plain border.

Using this width measurement, cut four pieces of plain fabric the same lengths as the check strips.

Construction - Blanket

1. Making the border

Unpin the check frame. With right sides together and raw edges even, pin one plain strip to the corresponding check strip along the long inner edge *(diag 4)*.

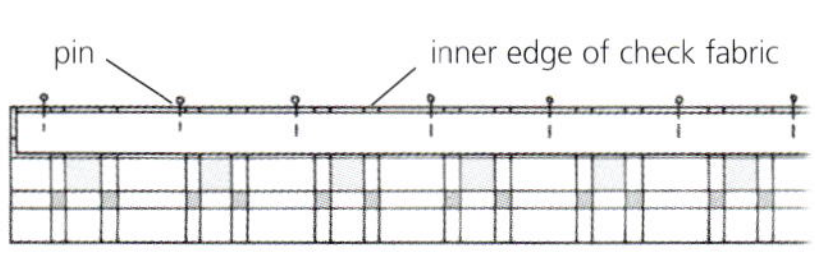

Diag 4

Stitch the two pieces together. Press the seam to one side.

Turn under and press 1cm (3/8") on the remaining long raw edge of the plain fabric.

Repeat for the remaining three sides.

2. Mitred corners

Reposition the strips around the blanket, forming a rectangular frame as before *(diag 5)*.

Diag 5

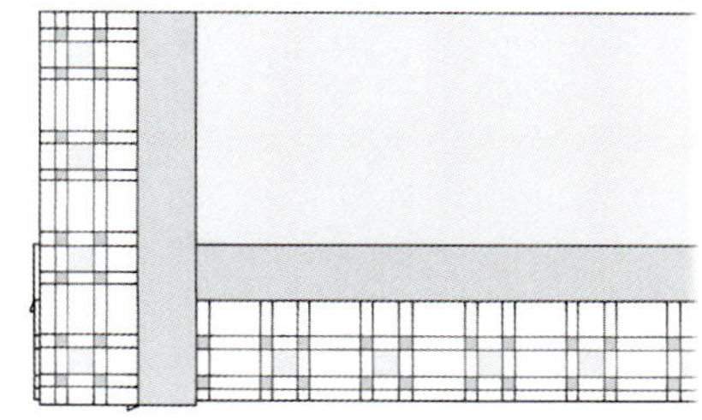

With checks matching at the corners, diagonally fold the ends under. Press the folds *(diag 6)*.

Diag 6

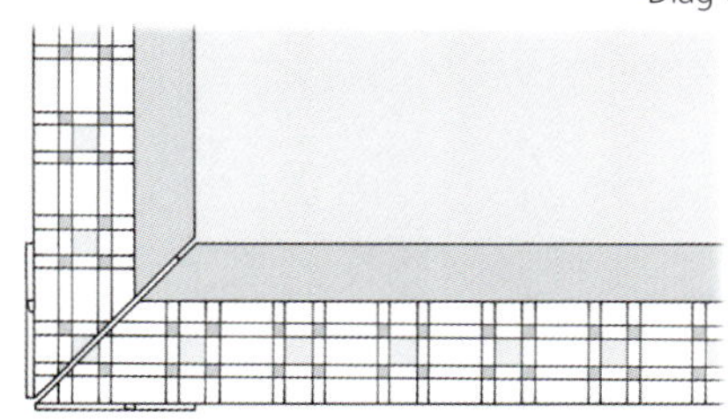

With right sides together and matching the pressed diagonal lines, lay the corresponding strips for one corner together.

Pin and stitch along the diagonal fold line, stopping at the inner stitch line *(diag 7)*.

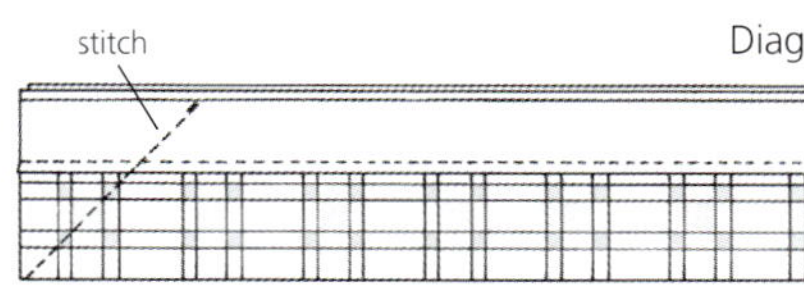

Diag 7

Trim the seams to 1cm (3/8") and press open. Repeat for the remaining corners.

3. Attaching the piping

Follow Step 4 of Construction Method 1 on page 135 to attach the piping to the inside edge of the frame.

Pin and stitch the piping to the outer edge of the frame in the same manner.

4. Attaching the border

With right sides together and raw edges even, pin one long inner edge of the frame to one long side of the blanketing. Stitch along the piping stitch line, beginning and ending at the diagonal seam *(diag 8)*. Repeat

Diag 8

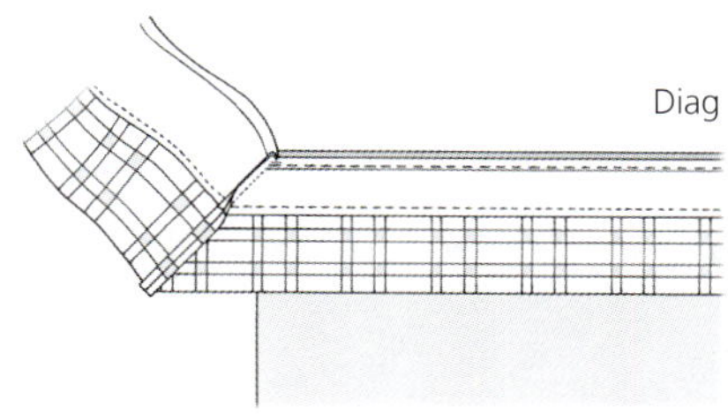

for the adjacent end, ensuring that the previously attached border is held out of the way. Repeat for the remaining side and end.

Press the border away from the blanket. On the right side, topstitch along the plain border close to the piping *(diag 9)*.

Diag 9

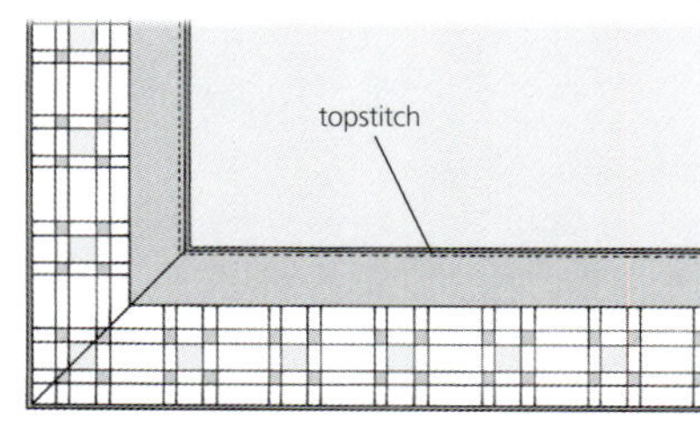

5. Attaching the backing

Cut one piece of backing and one piece of wadding to the same size as the framed blanket.

Lay the wadding on a flat surface. Place the blanket, right side up, over the wadding. Pin the layers together ensuring they are smooth. Working outwards from the centre, tack the layers in a grid. Tack around all four sides 3cm (1 1/4") in from the raw edges of the blanket *(diag 10)*.

Diag 10

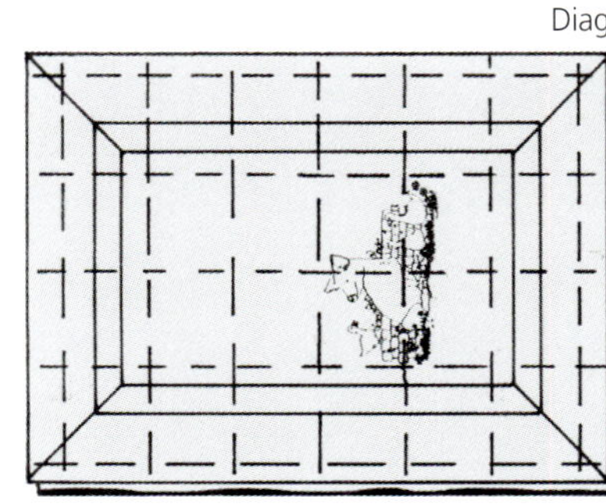

With right sides together and raw edges even, place the blanket over the backing. Pin the layers together around the outer edge. Stitch, following the previous piping stitch line, leaving a 20cm (8") opening in one side.

Trim the wadding seam allowance and clip the corners. Turn through to the right side and press. Turn under the seam allowance on the opening and hand stitch closed. Press.

Construction - Bag

1. Buttonhole

Fold the bag in half along the upper edge and finger press the fold. Measure down the fold line for 8cm (3 1/4") and mark. Measure down a further 2cm (3/4") and mark. Work a machine buttonhole between the marks *(diag 1)*.

Diag 1

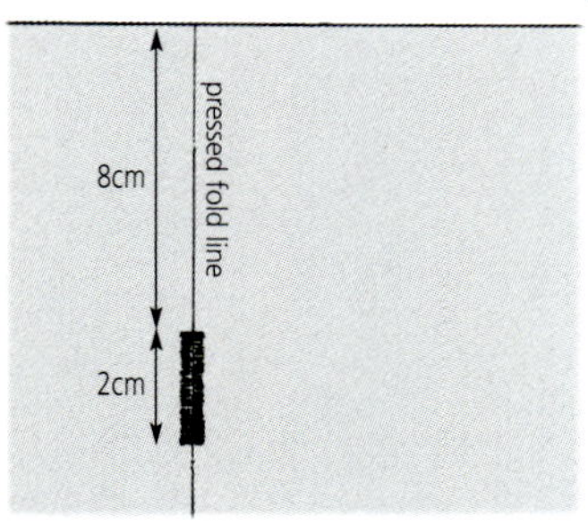

2. Attaching the embroidered piece

When the embroidery is complete, cut the rectangle out along the marked cutting lines.

Follow Step 4 in Construction Method 1 on page 138 for attaching the piping to the rectangle.

Tack the piping in place. Machine stitch around all four sides along the piping stitch line, pivoting at the corners.

Press under the seam allowance on all sides. Centre the panel onto the bag 5cm (2") up from the lower edge. Pin and ditch stitch to attach, referring to Construction Method 1 on page 139 *(diag 16)*.

3. Centre back seam

With right sides together and raw edges even, pin the sides of the fabric together. Stitch, forming a tube. Press the seam open. Using the seam as one quarter mark, divide the lower edge into quarters and mark with pins *(diag 2)*.

Diag 2

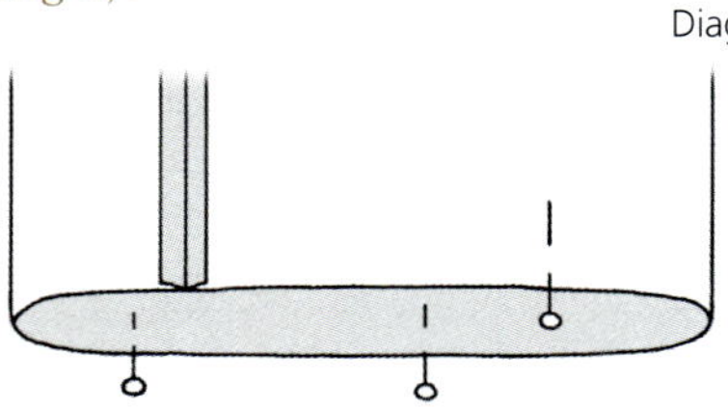

4. Straps

With right sides together and raw edges even, fold one strap in half lengthwise. Stitch down the long side and turn through. Repeat for the second strap.

Cut the thick piping cord into two pieces and thread into each strap. Position it so that the strap is longer than the cord at each end to reduce bulk.

Pin one strap 15cm (6") down from the upper edge and 5cm (2") away from the centre back seam. The seam is centred, facing out. Stitch *(diag 3)*.

Diag 3

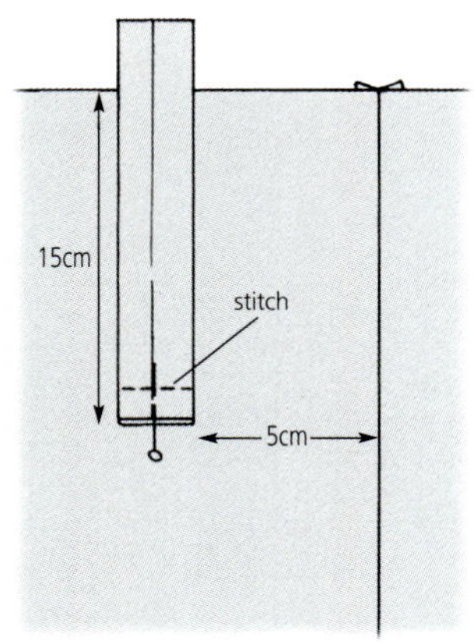

Fold the strap downwards and topstitch *(diag 4)*.

Pin the remaining end of the strap 5cm (2") away from the centre back seam on the lower edge of the bag. Stitch *(diag 5)*.

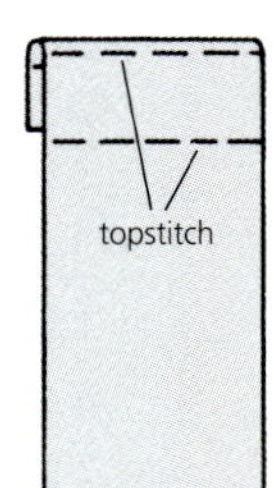

Diag 4

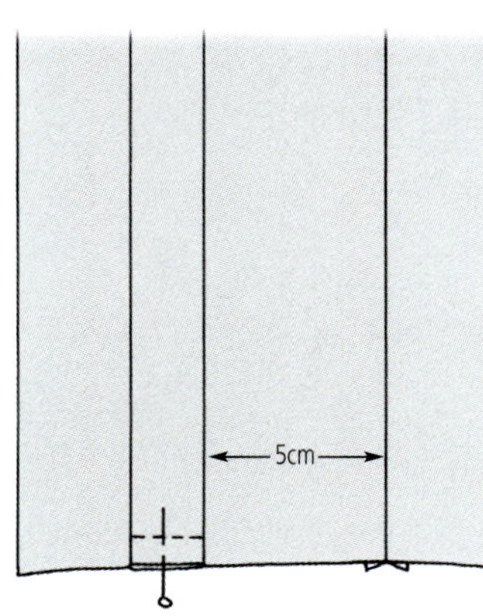

Diag 5

Repeat for the remaining strap. Turn the bag to the wrong side.

5. Joining the base

Mark the outer edge of the base into quarters.

Matching pins and with right sides together, pin the base into the bag. The straps are sandwiched between *(diag 6)*. Stitch.

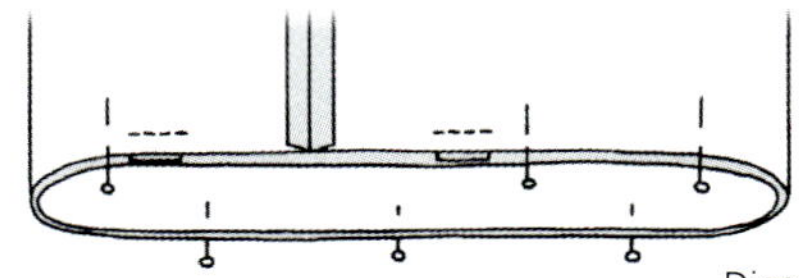

Diag 6

6. Forming the lining

Make the lining in the same manner as the bag, omitting the straps and leaving a 15cm (6") opening in the centre back seam. Turn the lining right side out.

7. Joining the bag and lining

With right sides together and upper edges even, place the lining inside the bag, matching the centre back seams. Pin and stitch around the upper edge.

Turn to the right side through the opening in the lining. Turn under the seam allowance and hand stitch the opening closed *(diag 7)*. Push the lining into the bag, with the upper seam line 5cm (2") from the upper edge of the bag. Tack in place *(diag 8)*.

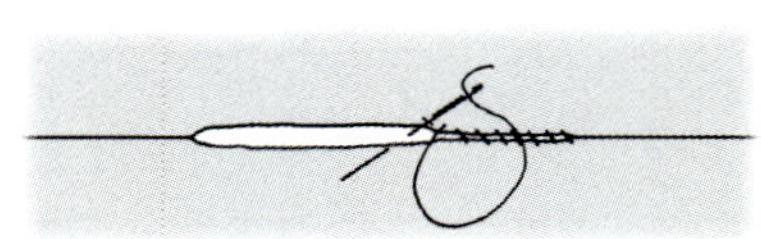

Diag 7

Diag 8

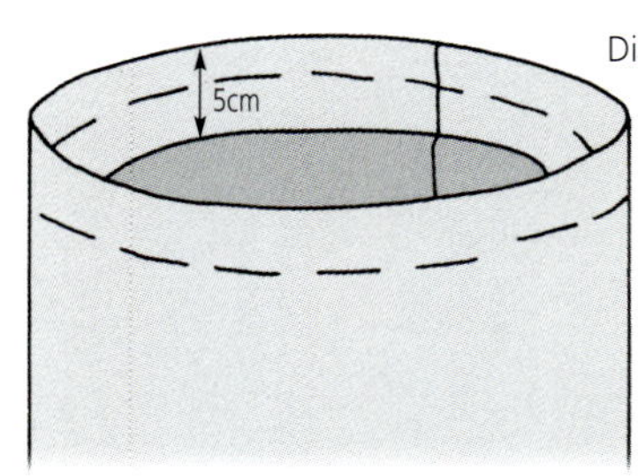

Press, ensuring the seam allowance faces towards the lining.

8. Forming the casing

On the right side, measure and mark a line 2cm (3/4") from the upper edge. Stitch along the marked line. Stitch a second row 2cm (3/4") below the first, noting that the two rows are either side of the buttonhole *(diag 9)*.

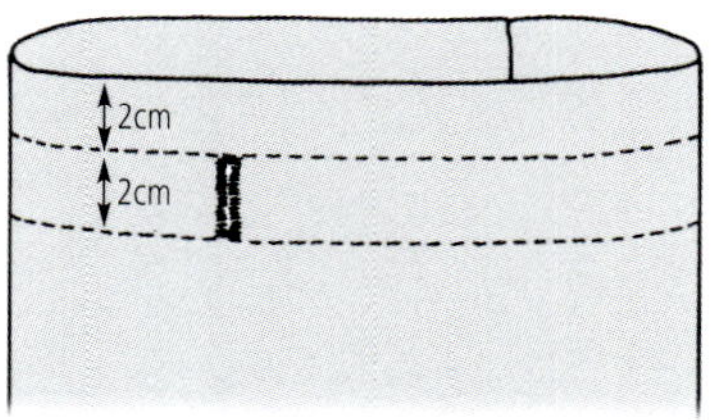

Diag 9

9. Finishing

Fold the green cord in half. Beginning and ending at the buttonhole, thread the folded end of the cord through the casing. Cut the fold in the cord and knot the cut ends together. Knot the remaining ends together in a similar manner *(diag 10)*.

Diag 10

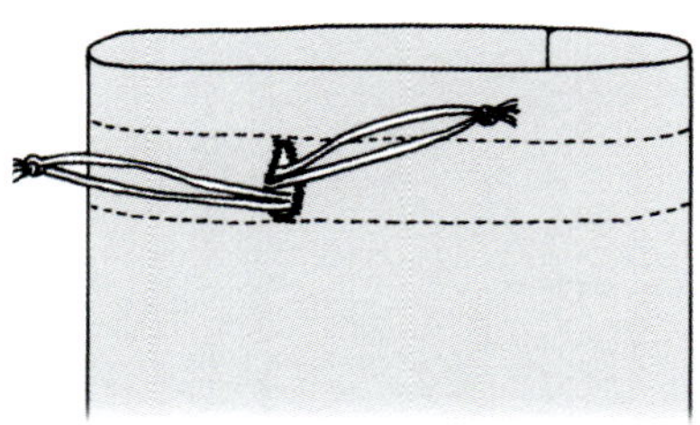

MAKING PIPING

A simple way of decorating the edge of a blanket is with the addition of piping. It can be purchased ready made, or alternatively can be made by covering cord with strips of fabric chosen to complement the blanket.

1. Preparing the strips

Cut enough bias strips to cover the length of piping cord.

With right sides together and matching raw edges, pin and stitch the ends of two strips together *(diag 1)*.

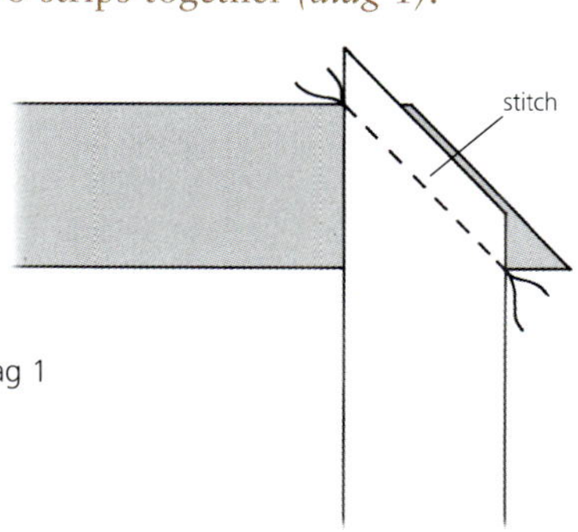

Diag 1

Attach the remaining strips in the same manner to form one long strip. Press the seams open.

2. Covering the cord

Place the piping cord along the centre on the wrong side of the strip *(diag 2)*.

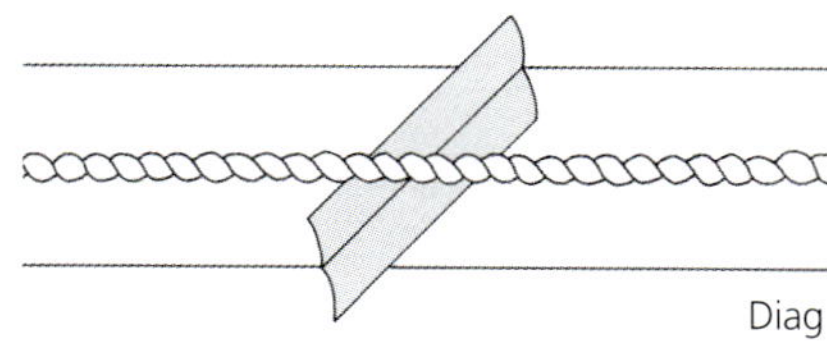

Diag 2

With wrong sides together, fold the strip in half along the length, enclosing the cord. Using a suitable presser foot, stitch through both layers of fabric as close as possible to the cord *(diag 3)*.

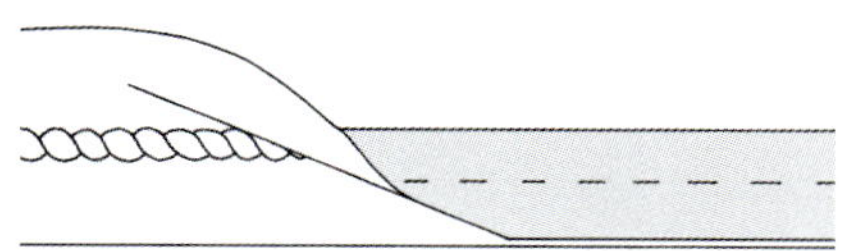

Diag 3

CONSTRUCTION METHOD 1 – PIPED BINDING

1. Preparation

When the embroidery is complete, remove any tacking threads or water-soluble pen marks which may still be visible through the embroidery. Place the embroidered fabric face down on a well padded surface and press. Do not press over any section which has raised embroidery.

2. Attaching the backing

A) With the wrong side uppermost, spread the backing fabric out flat. If the blanket you are working on requires the use of wadding, centre it over the backing. With the right side uppermost, place the embroidered blanket over the wadding or simply over the backing. Pin the layers together ensuring they are smooth. Working outwards from the centre, tack the layers together in a grid *(see diag 1)*.

B) Tack around the four sides 3cm (1 1/4") in from the raw edges of the blanket *(diag 1)*.

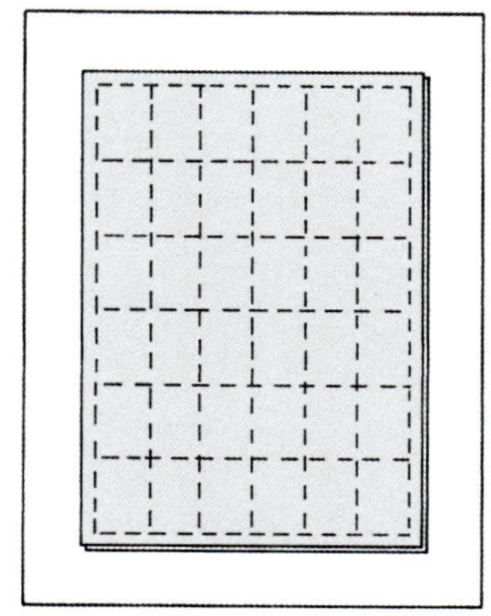

Diag 1

C) With the blanket uppermost, fold in and press 1cm (3/8") on all sides of the backing fabric *(diag 2)*.

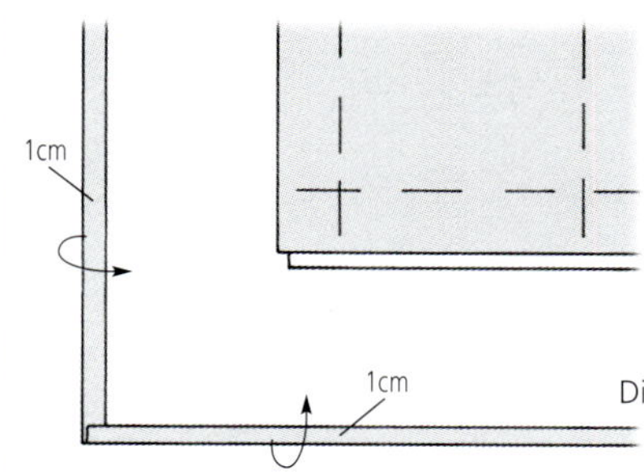

Diag 2

Fold in and press the remaining fabric, so that the backing fits firmly around the edges of the blanket *(diag 3)*.

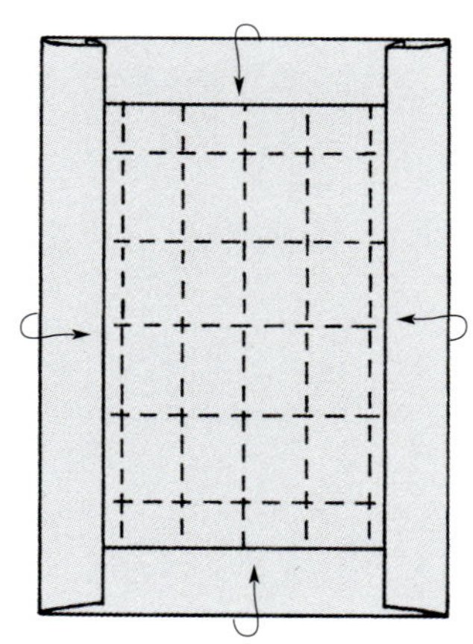

Diag 3

Unfold the backing fabric.

3. Forming the mitred corners

Diagonally fold in one corner of the backing so that it folds on the exact corner of the blanket. Ensure the pressed fold lines are aligned with the edges of the blanket. Press along the diagonal fold line *(diag 4)*.

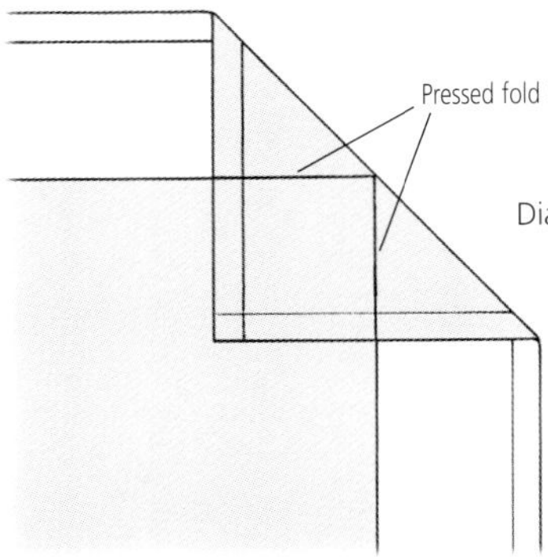

Diag 4

Open out the corner. With right sides together and matching raw edges, fold the corner back on itself and match the pressed diagonal fold lines and pin. Stitch along the diagonal fold line, stopping 1cm (3/8") away from the raw edge *(diag 5)*.

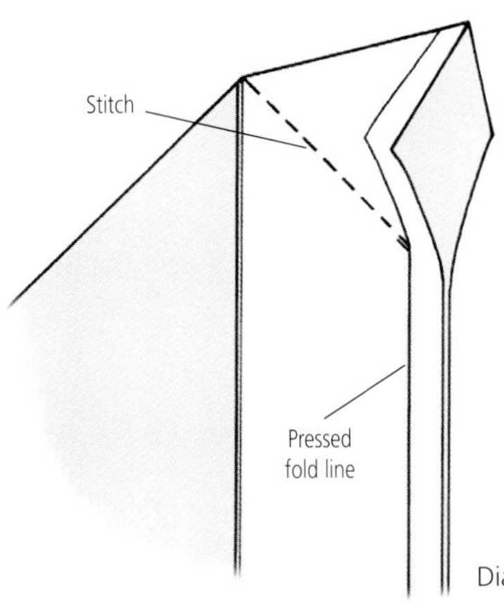

Diag 5

Trim the diagonal seam leaving a 1cm (3/8") seam allowance and then trim across the corner *(diag 6)*.

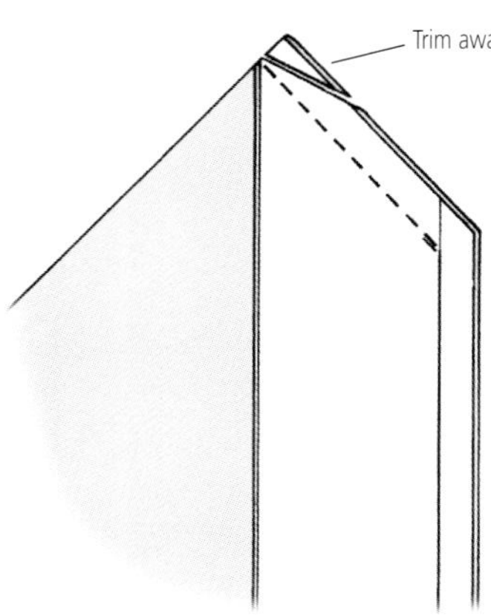

Diag 6

Press the seam open. Repeat on the remaining corners. Turn the backing to the right side creating a binding. Ensure that the blanket is flat inside the mitred corner.

4. Attaching the piping

Begin and end with the piping at the centre of the lower edge. With right sides together and matching raw edges, pin the piping to the binding. Leave a 5cm (2") tail extending past the centre point *(diag 7)*.

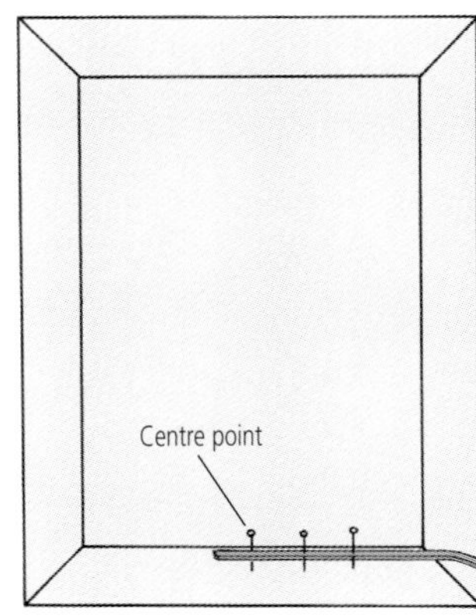

Diag 7

When reaching the first corner clip the piping heading into the corner point *(diag 8)*.

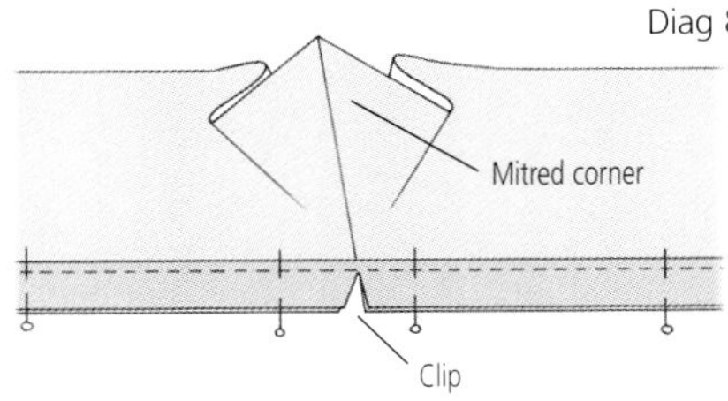

Diag 8

Continue pinning the piping in the same manner until reaching the beginning.

Trim any excess length of piping allowing a 5cm (2") tail to overlap.

Lay the ends of the piping side by side and mark each end with a pin at the centre point of the binding. Unpick the stitching on the piping for 4cm (1 5/8") away from the pin marks on both ends *(diag 9)*.

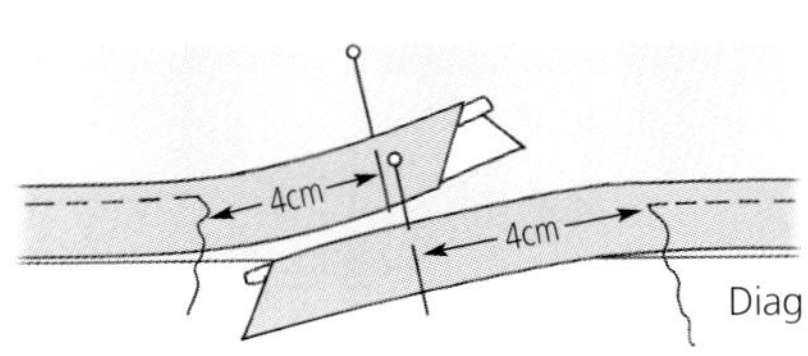

Diag 9

Uncover the piping cord back to the stitching on both ends. Wrap sewing thread around the cord for approximately 6mm (1/4") beginning at the centre point at each end *(diag 10)*.

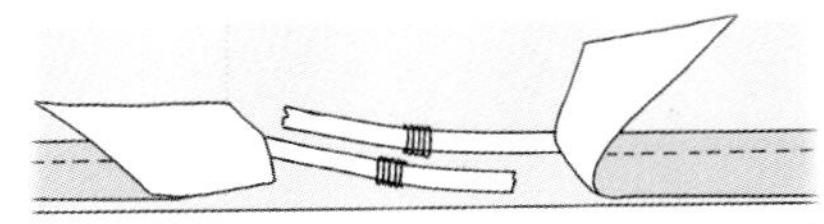
Diag 10

Trim away the excess length of piping cord on both ends *(diag 11)*.

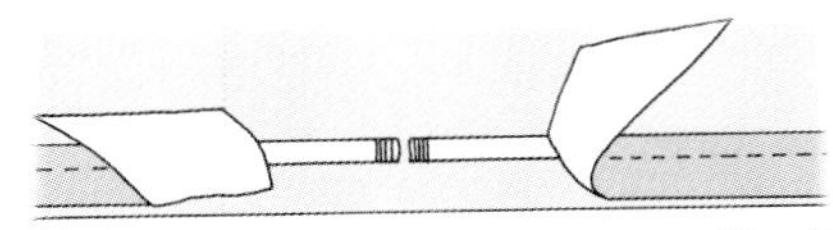
Diag 11

Open out the ends of the bias strips and measure a 1cm (3/8") seam allowance beyond the pin marks. Cutting along the straight grain (diagonally across the strip) trim away the excess lengths of fabric *(diag 12)*.

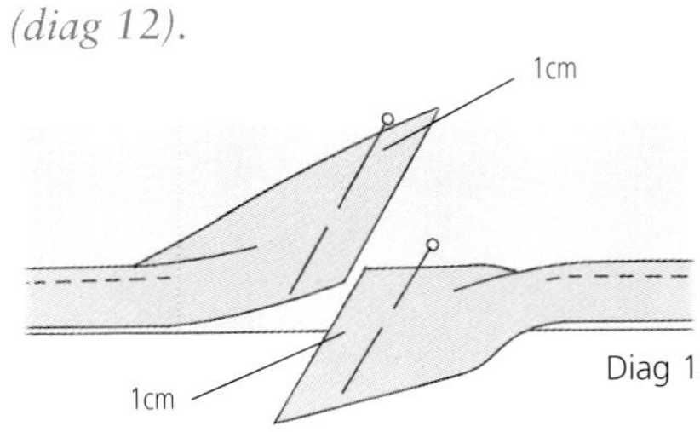

Diag 12

With right sides together, place one end at right angles over the other end. Stitch along the stitch line *(diag 13)*.

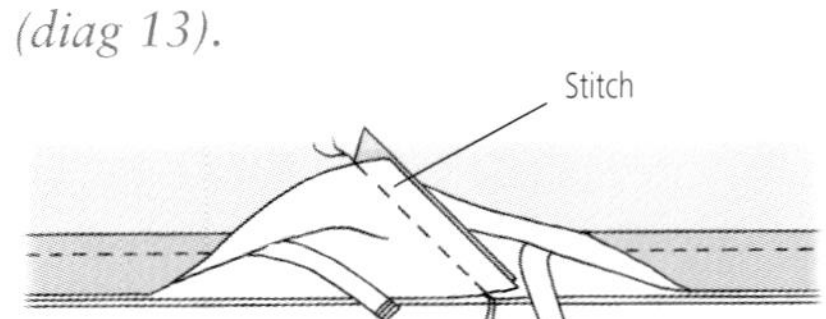

Diag 13

Press the seam open. With the cord ends butting each other, refold the bias strip over the cord and restitch *(diag 14)*.

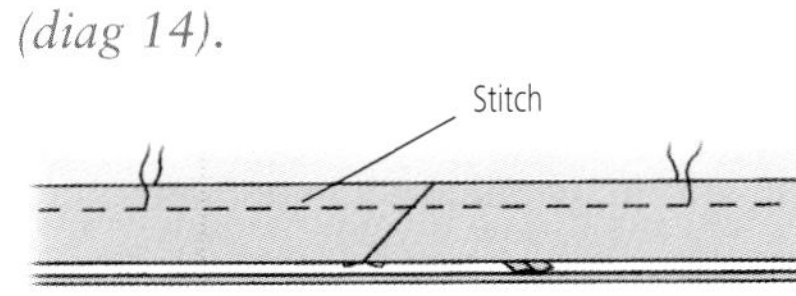

Diag 14

Stitch along the piping stitch line.

5. Finishing

Refold the inner edge seam allowance and press.

Pin the binding to the blanket along all sides. Using a machine sewing thread to match the backing fabric, top stitch the binding in place through all layers.

Stitch close to the folded edge and pivot at the corners *(diag 15)*.

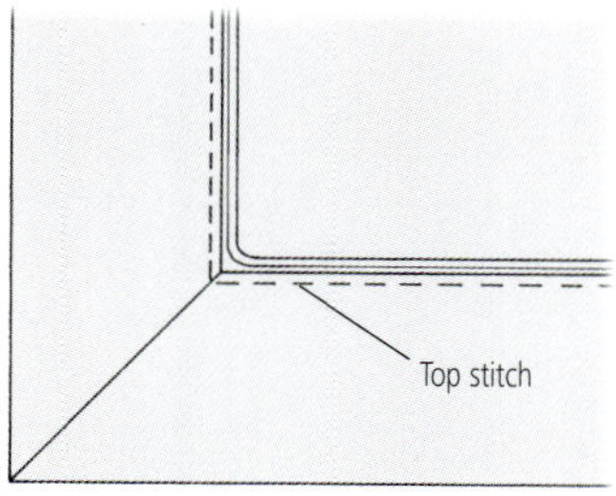

Diag 15

An alternative to top stitching is to stitch in the ditch close to the piping *(diag 16)*.

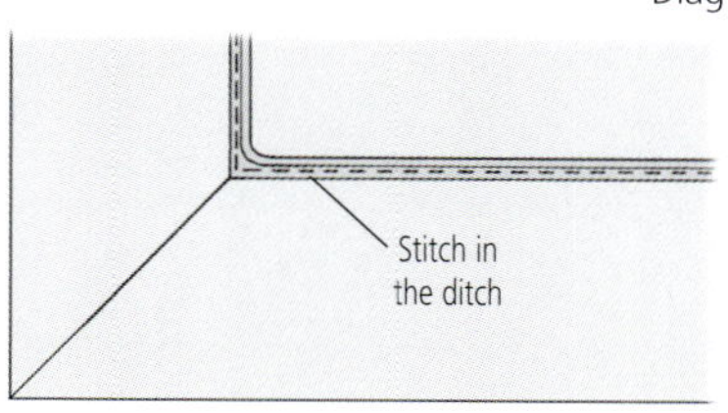

Diag 16

Remove all tacking threads from the blanket and carefully press the binding.

CONSTRUCTION METHOD 2 – SEPARATE BINDING

1. Preparation and attaching the backing

Follow steps 1 to 2b of Construction Method 1. Note that the backing does not extend past the edges of the blanket.

2. Attaching the binding

Turn under 1cm (3/8") on both long edges of each binding strip and press. With wrong sides together fold in half along the length and press. While folded, measure the finished width of the binding and deduct 1cm (3/8") *(diag 1)*.

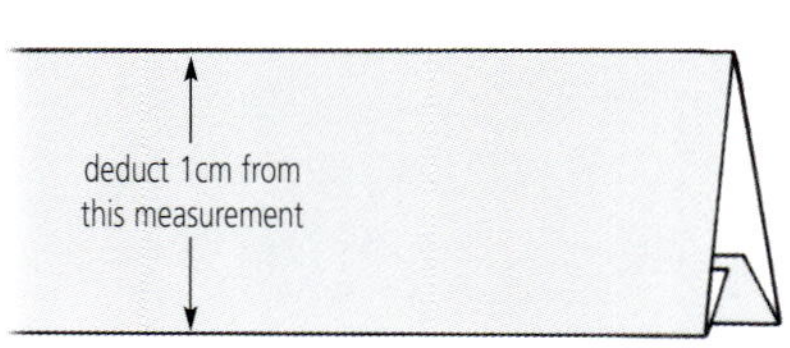

Diag 1

Using this new measurement, on the blanket measure in from the raw edges and rule a chalk line around all four sides *(diag 2)*.

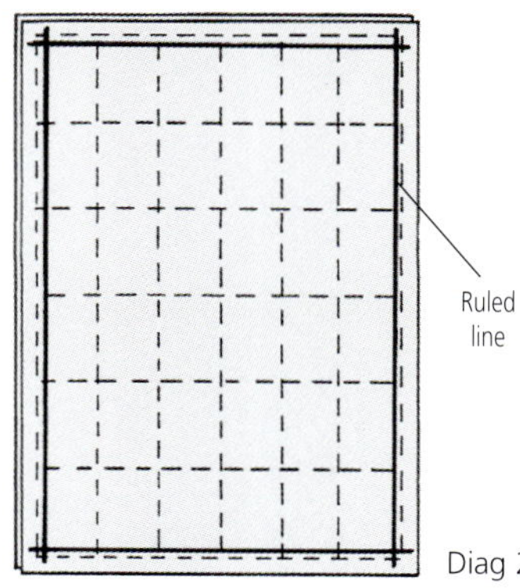

Diag 2

Unfold the binding. Centre a shorter piece of the binding along a corresponding end of the blanket. With right sides together, and aligning the raw edge of the binding with the ruled chalk line, pin and tack the binding through all layers beginning 15cm (6") away from the first corner *(diag 3)*.

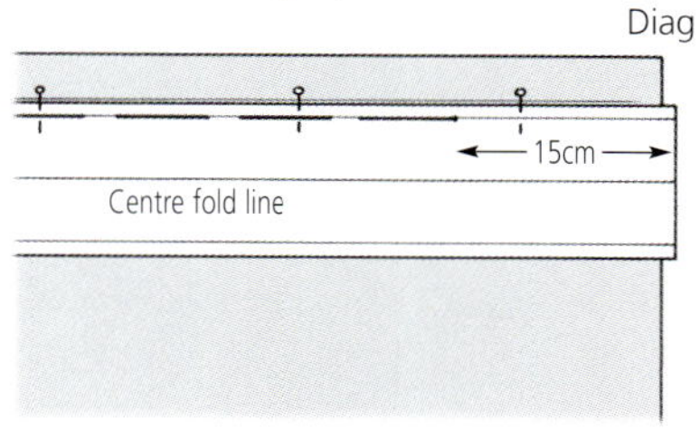

Diag 3

Tack to within 15cm (6") of the next corner. Attach the remaining end and the two sides in the same manner. Stitch. Press the binding away from the blanket.

3. Forming the mitred corners

Using a pin, mark the exact point where the centre fold line of the binding meets the corner of the blanket *(diag 4)*.

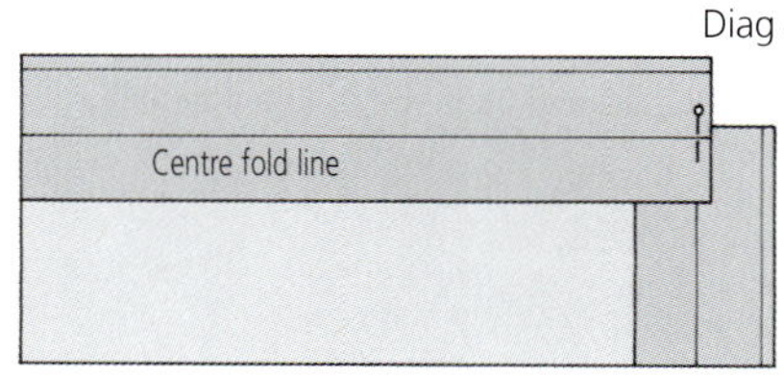

Diag 4

Repeat on the adjacent strip for this corner.

Place the two ends with right sides together, aligning the pins. Tack with tiny stitches *(diag 5)*.

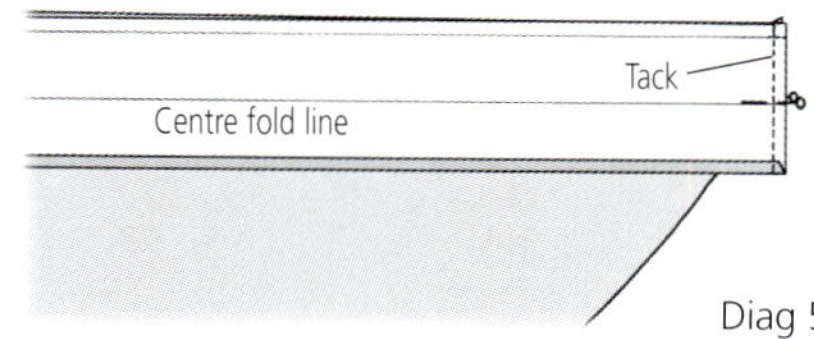

Diag 5

Fold the binding over so the tacking aligns with the centre fold line. Press the diagonal fold *(diag 6)*.

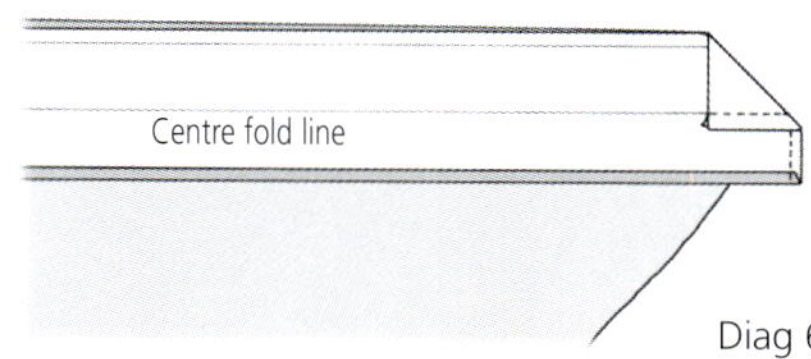

Diag 6

Unfold the corner and repeat for the second half.

Beginning and ending at the fold lines, tack and stitch along the diagonal fold lines, pivoting at the point *(diag 7)*.

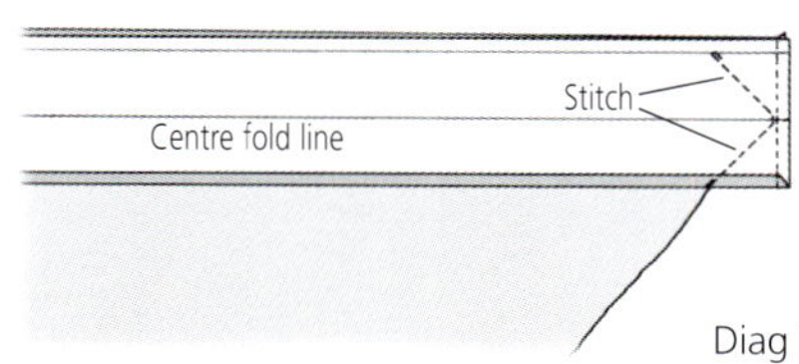

Diag 7

Trim the seams and clip across the point. Complete stitching the binding to the corner of the blanket, pivoting at the mitred corner. Form the mitres on the remaining corners in the same manner.

4. Finishing

Turn the mitred corners to the right side. Place the corners of the blanket into each of the corners of the binding. Refold the seam allowance around the remaining long edge of the binding and pin to the backing. Hand stitch, just covering the previous stitch line *(diag 8)*.

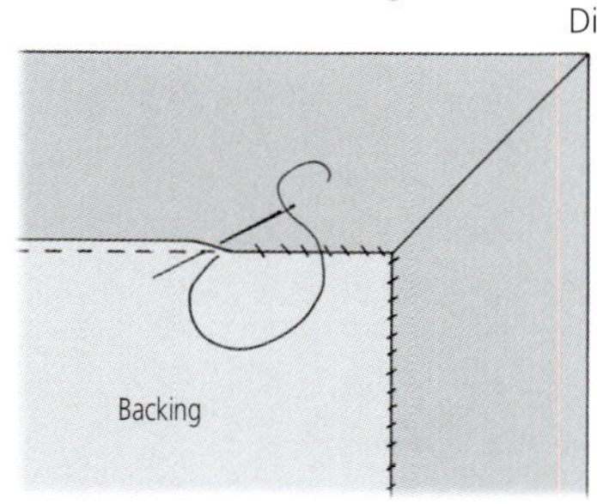

Diag 8

Remove all tacking threads and carefully press the binding.

INDEX

The Designers

Special thanks to our talented contributors who have made this book possible.

Kris Richards

Always an enthusiastic seamstress, Kris discovered embroidery ten years ago and now loves to combine her two passions. Her inspiration comes from old fashioned gift cards and wrapping, wallpapers and china, and of course her garden. "I always carry a pen and paper, just in case!" says Kris. She has embroidered hundreds of bullion roses and still finds new ways to incorporate them in her designs. Pastel colours worked on soft, creamy fabrics or light voiles are her favourites.

Annie Humphris

Annie has been a regular contributor to *Inspirations* magazine since the first issue, as well as the A-Z series. A passionate embroiderer and teacher, she held classes and weekend workshops at her farm in the Barossa Valley, South Australia, for nine years and has tutored at *Beating Around the Bush*. Annie's inspiration for the windflowers on her glorious blanket came from her own garden.

Helen Eriksson

An author and designer, Helen is one of Adelaide's most popular teachers. Until recently she had her own shop where she conducted classes and now continues to teach at home. Her lavish ribbon embroidery designs are the subject of her book, *Ribbon Renaissance,* published in 1999. Wool embroidery, however, is Helen's first love. Capturing the subtlety of colour and texture with a variety of threads and yarns is a challenge she enjoys.

Jenny McWhinney

Ever since her first blanket appeared in *Inpirations* so many years ago, Jenny has had a devoted *Country Bumpkin* following and has recently published her own book. It is easy to see that Jenny's inspiration comes from nature - in fact she says that her own garden is a constant source of ideas with all the Australian native birds and animals that live there or visit at different times of the year.

Carolyn Pearce

A regular contributor to *Inspirations,* Carolyn has embroidered some of our most popular blankets. *Fruits of the Hedgerow* introduced some of the raised effects that Carolyn has continued to develop over the years in *Lavender Fields* and *Bouquet of Flowers,* culminating in the wondrous *Hedgerow Flowers.* Carolyn's delight in embroidering is obvious in the meticulous way in which she creates every element of her design. Her use of a variety of threads of different weight and texture captures the play of light and helps to achieve a sense of depth.

Julie Graue

One of *Country Bumpkin's* best-loved designers, Julie is famous for her exquisitely smocked and embroidered children's garments. She teaches regularly, encouraging novices to become accomplished and addicted needleworkers. *Posies,* stitched in her favourite colours, is typical of the soft and pretty style of so many of her projects.

Libby Vater

Having dabbled in numerous artistic areas, Libby found that her interest in embroidery soon became a passion. She had been embroidering for only three years when her first blanket, *The Woolly Sheep* appeared in *Inspirations,* issue 18. While she attributes her artistic talents to her grandmother, an avid gardener, painter and floral artist, Libby thanks her mother for encouraging her to design her own projects. It is the versatility of embroidery with all its many facets which appeals to Libby.

Susan O'Connor

Susan is a contributor, teacher and editor at *Country Bumpkin.* Known for the perfection she achieves in design and workmanship, Susan has created many memorable projects for both *Inspirations* and *AS&E.* Her background in fine arts and drawing and her love of threads and textiles are obvious in all her work, from heirloom garments to raised Elizabethan work and lush woollen blankets.

Debbie Shepherd

Debbie grew up in Adelaide surrounded by family members 'creating treasures'. Her inspiration is the Elizabethan era - she is sure that she once sat at her embroidery in a castle, surrounded by rich furnishings, a basket of gold threads at her side. An accomplished designer of both smocked garments and embroidered blankets, Debbie believes there are endless ways of embellishing with threads and ribbons.

Other Publications from Country Bumpkin

If you would like more information on any Country Bumpkin title, please contact:

Country Bumpkin Publications
PO Box 194, Kent Town, South Australia, 5071, Australia
Within Australia: Phone: (08) 8363 4544 Fax: (08) 8363 4595
Outside Australia: Phone: +61 8 8363 4544 Fax: +61 8 8363 4595
www.countrybumpkin.com.au

The A-Z Series

Over 1,000,000 sold worldwide. The ultimate reference books for needleworkers.

A-Z of Embroidery Stitches

A-Z of Smocking

A-Z of Bullions

A-Z of Wool Embroidery

A-Z of Embroidered Flowers

A-Z of Ribbon Embroidery

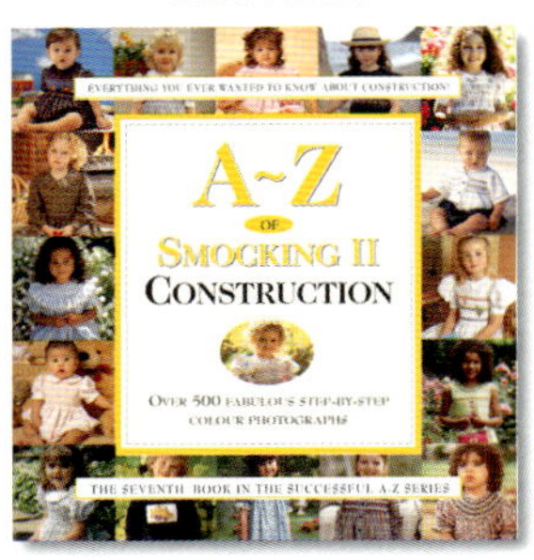

A-Z of Smocking II

Needlework Books

Filled with beautiful projects, easy instructions, superb photography and full size patterns.

Inspirations Baby

Inspirations Gifts

Inspirations Bridal

Magazines Published Quarterly

Inspirations

Australian Smocking and Embroidery

country bumpkin

Stockists

country bumpkin

Country Bumpkin Shop
53 The Parade, Norwood, SA 5067
Phone 08 8363 9822
Fax 08 8363 9833

For your mail order requirements please contact
Email mailorder@countrybumpkin.com.au
Phone 08 8363 4544
PO Box 194 Kent Town SA 5067

SEMCO
Design Quality Value

Please contact Semco Crafts for your local stockist details

Anchor

Exclusive distributor of Anchor Threads in Australia and New Zealand

AUSTRALIA
Unit 4, 7-11 Parraweena Rd
Taren Point NSW 2229
Phone 61 2 8543 4300
Toll Free 1800 641 277

NEW ZEALAND
33c Sir William Ave
East Tamaki, Auckland
Phone 64 9 273 8040
Toll Free: 0800 805 775

www.semco.com.au

Presencia
AUSTRALIA

PO Box 134, Mitchell, ACT 2911
ristal@austarmetro.com.au
Ph 02 6241 2293 Fax 02 6241 8382

Ben Britim Distributors
WHOLESALERS OF QUALITY NEEDLEWORK
ABN 25 078 825 055

Available at your nearest specialist needlework store.

Aussie Heirlooms
Wholesale suppliers of mini piping
Made in Australia

Email: aussieheirlooms@hotmail.com
3 Poplar Street, West Beach,
South Australia 5024 Australia
Phone/Fax (Int. 61) (08) 8353 0415

The Luxury of Rajmahal

182 High Street, Kangaroo Flat
Victoria 3555 Australia
www.rajmahal.com.au
Tel 03 5447 7699
International Tel 61 3 5447 7699
Fax 03 5447 7899
International Fax 61 3 5447 7899

---

design the future
MADEIRA
Call SSS Pty Ltd on:
1300 887 072
for your nearest stockist

CREATIVE WORLD
DMC

Radda Pty Ltd
51-55 Carrington Road
Marrickville NSW 2204
P.O. Box 317
Earlwood NSW 2206 Australia
Phone 61 2 9559 3088
Fax 61 2 9559 5338
Email cservice@radda.com.au

Kacoonda

Hand dyed 4, 7, 13 and 32mm silk ribbons with complimenting wool, mohair and silk embroidery threads. For wholesale enquiries or nearest stockist contact:

Phone: 03 9776 7438 Fax: 03 9776 5698
Email: kacoonda@netstra.com.au

IRELAND NEEDLECRAFT
PTY. LTD. (Inc. in Vic.) ACN 700 210 568

Appletons Crewel Wool, Paterna Persian Wool, The Thread Gatherer Sheep's Wool, Mill Hill Beads and Kreinik Threads are distributed by

Ireland Needlecraft Pty Ltd
PO Box 1175, Narre Warren DC, Victoria 3805
Phone: 61 3 9702 3222 Fax 61 3 9702 3255
Email: enquiries@irelandneedlecraft.com.au
Website: www.irelandneedlecraft.com.au

Minnamurra
THREADS
SIMPLY STUNNING

PO Box 374 Glebe NSW 2037 Australia
Phone/Fax +61 02 9570 7004

AU VER À SOIE

PO Box 134, Mitchell, ACT 2911
ristal@austarmetro.com.au
Ph 02 6241 2293 Fax 02 6241 8382

GEELONG BLANKET COMPANY

Manufacturers and Wholesalers of Wool Blanket Fabric, Cashmere, Doctors Flannel and Fine Wool Fabric

143 Church Street, Geelong West
Victoria 3218 Australia
Ph: (03) 5277 2006 Fax: (03) 5277 1925
www.geelongblanketcompany.com.au

COTTON ON CREATIONS

Unit 2, 52 Govetts Leap Road
Blackheath NSW 2785 AUSTRALIA
Ph: (02) 4787 6588 Fax: (02) 4787 6544
Email: cottononcreations@bigpond.com.au
Wholesale only. Business credentials required.
Agents in all states.

Colour Streams
HAND DYED SILKS
EMBROIDERY THREADS, RIBBONS, KITS & PATTERNS

Robyn Alexander
5 Palm Avenue, Mullumbimby
NSW 2482 Australia
Ph/Fax 61 2 6684 2577
Email: colourstreams@ozemail.com.au
www.colourstreams.com.au

KIRRA YARNS

PO Box 134, Mitchell, ACT 2911
ristal@austarmetro.com.au
Ph 02 6241 2293 Fax 02 6241 8382